FULL CONTACT KARATE TRAIN

This book is dedicated to my parents.
Regrettably, my father did not
live to experience it.

J.

Juergen Hoeller & Axel Maluschka

FULL CONTACT KARATE TRAINING

Meyer & Meyer Sport

Original title: Vollkontakt-Karate-Training
© Meyer & Meyer Verlag, 2010

FULL CONTACT KARATE TRAINING

Hoeller/Maluschka
Maidenhead: Meyer & Meyer Sport (UK) Ltd., 2011
ISBN: 978-1-84126-320-5

© 2011 by Meyer & Meyer Sport (UK) Ltd.
Auckland, Beirut, Budapest, Cairo, Cape Town, Dubai, Graz, Indianapolis, Maidenhead,
Melbourne, Olten, Singapore, Tehran, Toronto
Member of the World
Sport Publishers' Association (WSPA)
www.w-s-p-a.org
Printed by: B.O.S.S Druck und Medien GmbH
ISBN: 978-1-84126-320-5
E-Mail: info@m-m-sports.com
www.m-m-sports.com

Contents

Introduction by Semmy Schilt

(4 x K-1 Grand Prix Champion, 2 x Karate World Champion)

Several books have been written on the subject of Full Contact Karate, most of which have been about Kyokushin Karate, which was one of the pillars of full contact sports.

One of the spin-offs of Kyokushin Karate is the style I have been practicing for nearly twenty years now – Ashihara Karate.

Although there is little difference when competing in full contact tournaments, some of the styles have their own approach in training and exercises, and some of these spin-offs have gained a lot of interest because of their approach.

For me, it was the Sabaki movements and the ability to create realistic fighting situations that I found most appealing.

Full contact Karate has formed the basis for my success in several systems that I have learned and fought in.

I hope this book by Juergen Hoeller and Axel Maluschka contributes to the development of martial arts.

Semmy Schilt 6th Dan Ashihara International Karate
The Netherlands

Foreword by Dave Jonkers

Martial arts do have a rich history.

It not only shows in the many different styles they have, it also shows in the development within all of these styles.

Development in a young style like Ashihara International Karate is no exception to this. From the moment of its introduction in the 80s, many changes have been made by different style leaders and masters.

My student Semmy Schilt and I have developed our own experiences and knowledge in Ashihara International Karate.

Technical and strategical aspects that we used in Semmy's long career in the disciplines he fought, such as K-1, Pride, Pancrase and DaiDoJuka, were the basis of what we created in our style.

In the beginning of 1993, I met a German Taekwondo-Ka in one of the Ashihara training camps in the south of Holland. During these days of training he showed interest in the Ashihara style and we spoke about technical aspects, fighting strategy, etc.

I noticed that this guy had a lot of potential and was capable of judging things at a distance, in which he could criticize and analyse his and others' way of practice.

He introduced himself as Juergen Hoeller, a Taekwondo-Ka from Germany. Up to now I know Juergen as a person who is always busy with all kinds of studies and also a lecturer in the meantime.

A long time ago, it must have been in the late 70s, I was training with one of the top Judokas, Isao Okano, former Olympic Champion. I did some Uchi Komi (repeating techniques) and Okano approached me and asked me why I did my technique like that.

I just answered, "Because I learned it like this." Then he only said, "I thought you were more intelligent." I realized what he meant.

Everything you do has a reason.
Everything you teach should have an argument.
Analyze, and then try to criticize, and accept, change or improve it.

These are things that are accepted as normal in society, but because of the hierarchy in martial arts with all kinds of masters who each have their status, things often will be taken as they are.

And this is what impressed me about Juergen Hoeller. He is not the Budoka who only gives critical reflections on things like techniques and strategies, but he also shows the way and direction of improvement.

Last year I received his book *Taekwondo – Eine systematische Annäherung (Taekwondo – A systematic approach)* and was surprised by it contents.

So I'm convinced that this book will contribute to the development of Karate, and I hope that this book will be a contribution to both students and teachers in their martial arts development.

Dave Jonkers 7th Dan Ashihara International Karate, teacher of Semmy Schilt

Expressions of Thanks and Notes by the Authors

This book has been a do you mean meticulous? project. Back in 1998, Juergen began writing the first lines of it. Axel began to work on the manuscript in 2003. In the course of the ensuing years, the text and concepts grew and were changed, chucked out or reinstated. Finally, it was left, however, to many, many people who unerringly supported us authors so that it could be turned into a book. Therefore, hearty thanks are due to:

In Zuidlaren, Holland – Axel, Neal, Semmy, Harald, Juergen

- Semmy Schilt Shihan (6th Dan Ashihara International Karate) for his support in this project and for his "Introduction" in this book, as well as for his patience during the photo sessions.
- Neal Lange and Harald Koot for their work as models.
- Peter van Eyk (5th Dan Karate) for his untiring work as a model.
- Harry Assenmacher (3rd Dan Karate) who, at short notice, made his new dojo in Bonn available for the photo shoot there.
- Ralf and Jacqueline Engler for the loan of photo equipment.
- Oliver Suchan for his helpful and stylish critique of the manuscript.
- Regina Ney-Wilkens for her persevering assistance with the editing.
- Alexa Deutz – our editor at the Meyer & Meyer Publishing Company – for her patience, as well as Corinna Reinders and Kerstin Vonderbank for their doggedness and work on the graphics.
- Last, but not least, thanks go to Dave Jonkers (7th Dan Ashihara International Karate) for his support. He earns our heartfelt thanks for his "Foreword" and also for letting his pupils Semmy, Neal and Harald work with us. Also, we thank him for allowing us to use his dojo "Health & Budo Center" in Zuidlaren for photos.

Harald und Neal

In Bonn, Germany – Axel, Peter and Juergen

Without you all, this book would not be what it is!

Before we get on with business, we would like to make a few comments.

In the book, we often use the term "Full Contact Karate." Particularly in the first part of the book, we refer to Ashihara Full Contact Karate or Ashihara International Karate. This is a specialized full contact style that we both practice. It is a variation worked up from Kyokushin Karate that is, besides Muay Thai, the stimulus in the modern full contact scene.

Juergen dropped into Ashihara Karate by accident the early '90s. A book by Hideyuki Ashihara came into his hands in London. Juergen was enthralled with the style described and got into contact with people in Holland. There, he regularly practiced Full Contact Karate, and in 1996 he brought the style of Ashihara International Karate to his home country, Germany. Axel was one of the first pupils of the German training group.

Ashihara Full Contact Karate, with its training methods and effectiveness, can take on Thai boxing any time. Indeed, the Karate style is built upon the traditional Japanese theories (structure, politeness, sense of responsibility with partner and sensei, etc.).

On the surface, the traditional and the full contact styles are similar from a technical aspect. However, full contact demands other methods of training and fighting actions in order to be successful. Paradoxically, continuous training using the Contact style is kinder on the joints than the traditional style. Training is nearer to real fighting and this is what makes a lot of fun for us authors.

We hope you have fun with it also. Have a good time trying out the suggested techniques and training forms.

Juergen + Axel

1   The Theory of Full Contact Karate

1.1 The Difference Between Ashihara Full Contact Karate and Other Karate Styles

Ashihara Full Contact Karate is a modern martial art that has its roots in Japanese tradition. The style is modern because the technical element (Japanese *Ryu*) is open to various influences, new experiences and effective techniques. In Ashihara full contact, you reflect and experiment. In this way, it is always open to further developments. The philosophical, social element remains traditional. This tradition is carried on in the style but in an adapted form.

Our western, industrialized society gives us a completely different environment than that found in Japan's past. For this reason, we cannot just simply reflect Japanese traditions. We have to adapt them and change them slightly. In this way, we can fulfill our pupil's demands and simultaneously allow for the positive aspects of the traditional Japanese structures of human relationships (such as exercising politeness, showing respect for those with wisdom and experience, etc.).

Just what are the differences between Ashihara Full Contact Karate and other Karate styles?

In most Karate styles, the pupils' basic training (kihon) consists of traditional forms. On the other hand, they use the techniques for self-defense and kumite completely differently, particularly when they are applied to the full contact style. In other words, a pupil spends a lot of time training in things that he cannot use in real fighting or in self-defense. This way he loses a lot of time. (This, of course is rather irrelevant when one considers lifetime training.) Furthermore, the pupil develops (possibly) false expectations about the effectiveness of his techniques.

The kihon techniques can be viewed as a very abstract model of presentation and principles that have roots in a specific historical situation. In the case of Karate techniques, the situation looks like this: A person without a weapon seeks to gain victory over a person holding a sword. The *ikken-hissatsu* principle (literally translated as "one fist, certain death," or in other words: one hit, one kill) has its origin in these historical times.

Most of the styles, in which the techniques are performed in free air and involve a form of no contact, have no connection with reality. The statement that the techniques are too dangerous or are even deadly compensates them, and this is given as the reason for not being allowed to perform them any differently. In the opinion of the authors, this is pure ideology.

Ashihara full contact has made a complete break away from such ideological axioms. Every, and we mean every, movement practiced by the pupil must be usable in real fighting. From the first moment, the beginner learns movements that he can use in self-defense and competition. He learns to use and adapt techniques against partners of any size and weight. Only in this way can the pupil develop his skills. He learns how to be hit and loses any fear of being hit.

He develops his self-assertion. He executes all the techniques with full power against punching bags, lower arm protectors or coaching mitts without over-straining his joints. All elements of Ashihara Full Contact Karate are aimed at increasing fighting ability.

Even when a pupil is training the Ashihara Katas, he does this more in a sparring fashion. For this, one, two or even more partners attack him with full force. Although the training partners execute each Kata in a specific sequence, the pupil must continually adapt himself to take on the various partners. Each exercise partner has to punch and kick in varying degrees of force, rapidly, while being precisely accurate and changing over from low to high. Therefore, the pupil has to follow closely and be attentive so that he is in a position to forcibly deliver his own techniques and cushion those thrown at him by the partners.

All the movements in Ashihara Full Contact Karate are natural ones. Although it may appear paradoxical, Ashihara Full Contact Karate is a "safe" Karate style that can be practiced by people of any age. Ashihara Full Contact Karate is actually a full contact system, but one that is not based on the use of pure strength. It is rather a question of using developed legwork, controlling techniques and maneuvers to "get out of the attacker's way."

Ashihara Full Contact Karate is an open-ended system in the sense that nothing is seen as perfect or complete. Up-to-date knowledge from sports research is continuously being integrated into the training structure. The techniques are being adapted to satisfy the demands for an increase in the difficulty of actions in the full contact scene. In this process of continual development, Ashihara Full Contact Karate absorbs and uses influences from Muay Thai, Kyokushinkai, Jiuitsu and Aikido. In this way, Ashihara Full Contact Karate creates its own identity and meets the criteria, in every sense, to be called a "modern" form of martial art.

1.2 The History of the Ashihara Full Contact Form: Ashihara International Karate

As can be seen from the diagram on Page 17, most of the existing full contact styles stem from Kyokushin Karate founded by Mas Oyama. The technical repertoire of Kyokushin Karate, particularly the low kicks and knee punches, has been expanded by influences from Muay Thai. The particular training methods have led to training and fighting bouts in Kyokoshin representing a kind of "materiel attrition." The "materiel," in this case, is the fighter himself. At the end of the day, only a certain type of Karateka who is both extremely physically and mentally hardened will be successful. Because of this kind of training and fighting, many pupils ceased their training. The dropout quota was relatively high.

Hideyuki Ashihara originally was a 5th Dan Kyokushin Karate. He recognized the problems described above and founded his own style. Ashihara Karate is based on a concept of neutralizing and controlling attacks by opponents. Similar to Aikido and Judo, it is not a question of employing strength against strength. It is rather more a question of the fighter dodging an opponent's attack or diverting his force so that he can bring the opponent into an unfavorable position where he can apply a counterattack.

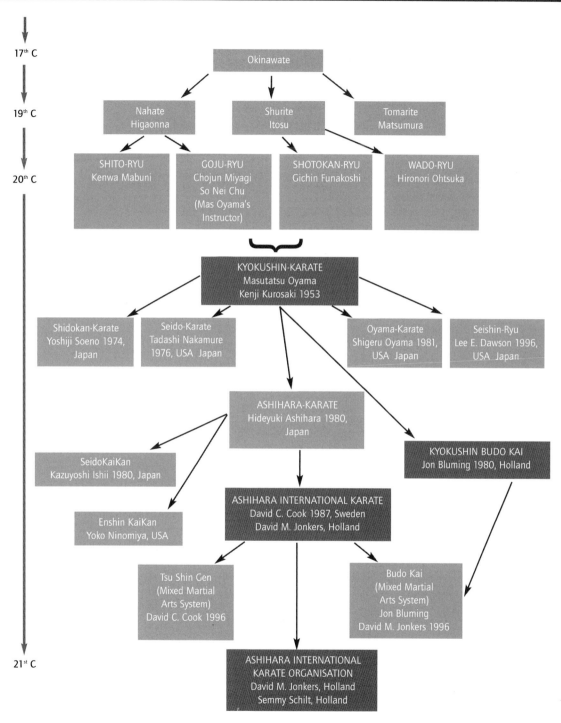

17th C

19th C

20th C

21st C

Okinawate

Nahate
Higaonna

Shurite
Itosu

Tomarite
Matsumura

SHITO-RYU
Kenwa Mabuni

GOJU-RYU
Chojun Miyagi
So Nei Chu
(Mas Oyama's
Instructor)

SHOTOKAN-RYU
Gichin Funakoshi

WADO-RYU
Hironori Ohtsuka

KYOKUSHIN-KARATE
Masutatsu Oyama
Kenji Kurosaki 1953

Shidokan-Karate
Yoshiji Soeno 1974,
Japan

Seido-Karate
Tadashi Nakamure
1976, USA Japan

Oyama-Karate
Shigeru Oyama 1981,
USA Japan

Seishin-Ryu
Lee E. Dawson 1996,
USA Japan

ASHIHARA-KARATE
Hideyuki Ashihara 1980,
Japan

SeidoKaiKan
Kazuyoshi Ishii 1980, Japan

KYOKUSHIN BUDO KAI
Jon Bluming 1980, Holland

Enshin KaiKan
Yoko Ninomiya, USA

ASHIHARA INTERNATIONAL KARATE
David C. Cook 1987, Sweden
David M. Jonkers, Holland

Tsu Shin Gen
(Mixed Martial
Arts System)
David C. Cook 1996

Budo Kai
(Mixed Martial
Arts System)
Jon Bluming
David M. Jonkers 1996

ASHIHARA INTERNATIONAL
KARATE ORGANISATION
David M. Jonkers, Holland
Semmy Schilt, Holland

Diagram 1: The origins of Ashihara International Karate

Ashihara International Karate as practiced today by Dave Jonkers and Semmy Schilt is known as a system that looks openly at new influences and techniques. Following the successes scored in K1, Pancrase, MMA, DaiDoJuka, etc., bouts by Ashihara Karatekas, such as Semmy Schilt, the technical elements of other styles have been absorbed and integrated into the Ashihara International Karate system. In this way, the style is continually being developed.

1.3   The Importance of Strategy and Tactics

In Full Contact Karate, the fighter's strategy and tactics are mechanisms that can help him come to terms successfully in a complex and uncertain situation. Because it contains many components that are not clearly defined and that are continually changing, the character of a fighting situation is complex. The fighter is only able to sense the situation in part and is poorly placed to control it efficiently. Strategy and tactics are in such cases "tools" for use in attempting to make a complex and chaotic situation clearer and more manageable. If both opponents are at the same level with regard to their technical prowess, fitness and mental preparation, the fighter who has the better strategy and (in relation to a concrete situation) tactics will be the winner. Using a clever strategy and tactics that only emphasize the strong sides and hide the weak points can also possibly lead to the weaker fighter ending up successful.

Generally, people are afraid of the unknown and are uncertain about the future. This fear can paralyze a fighter. This makes him possibly unable to act adequately both before and during a fight. As a result, the psychological facets of strategy and tactics are the elements that allow a fighter to create a structure out of the "chaos." He can read the situation better and exercise control in the important parts.

Strategy should be seen as depicted in the following plan of action either in a competition or real fight situation. The plan of action is dependent upon factors such as:
* Knowledge of the competition rules or – for street fighting – knowing that there are no rules that govern either fighter.
* Knowing one's own strengths and weaknesses and also those of the opponent (gained, for example, through video analysis, experience and observations regarding street fighting) concentrating totally on targeting (i.e., scanning) which points or regions are not protected or are vulnerable, etc.

A fighter can make decisions about upcoming bouts, because he knows himself and, whenever possible, he knows his opponent. This kind of preparation (or "homework") takes the strain off the fighter in a psychological sense. However, his anticipation must remain flexible. He should develop several strategies, in case of an injury or if he realizes that one of his strategies was based on false premises, information or expectations. However, there is the possibility the fighter may need to adapt his strategy ad hoc to the fight situation and he should ideally be ready to do this.

Let us summarize: We view strategy as an "internal" model of the fight sequence, or in other words, the development of a whole tournament or individual fight. While strategy has to be seen more as a general orientation guideline for tournaments or fights, tactics constitute the transformation of strategy into real fighting situations.

Using tactics, the fighter can successfully use his own techniques. He looks for the opponent's reactions using feints. He tries to discover any particular pattern of action used by his opponent, while at the same time keeping his own concealed. With the over-usage ("over-feeding") of feints, he tries to mislead the opponent, giving him false information, thereby causing his opponent to leave gaps in his defense that the fighter then uses to his advantage after sizing up the opponent. The fighter's aim is to take the lead in the fight and maintain control of this lead.

From this point of view, strategy, tactics and techniques form a hierarchy in which techniques only represent the moment of execution. By using an adequate strategy and tactical maneuvers, a fighter can actively create so-called tactical moments in which the opponent is practically helpless for a split second. Then, the fighter can put his techniques to use. However, for this, he will need a broad spectrum of knowledge and experience, a realistic assessment of his own capabilities and those of his opponent, and a good, resolute fighting spirit.

1.4 The Fight

1.4.1 The Complex Nature of a Fight Situation - The Difference Between Competition and Self-Defense

At first sight, a fight situation appears very chaotic and unstructured.

A sporting fight is limited by time, the actions that are allowed or disallowed, the restrictions of a defined fighting area and the presence of a referee. On the other hand, in street fighting, there are *no rules*! The person being attacked can choose neither the time, place nor weight of the attacker. As a result, a street fight is far more complex than a sporting bout because the nature and condition of the ground, lighting and overall vigilance all contribute to the possible outcome of the fight. In a street fight, you have to fight until you win or lose! In a street fight, you risk your health and possibly your life! In a sporting bout, if you lose, you are probably only going to dent your ego.

Without wanting to go into too many details, in this section we list some of the more important factors of a fight situation. The questions posed are meant only to get you to think about the complexity of a fight situation. The more questions a fighter asks himself, the more he knows about the factors a fight may entail and about his individual strengths and reactions (i.e., "how do you cope with an adrenaline rush under stress?").

By achieving this, he will be in a better situation to command a fight situation, whether it is in the ring or on the street.

What are the factors regarding the location?

- What room is there to maneuver? (Subway, soccer pitch, bout ring, etc.)
- What are the lighting conditions?
- What kind of surface is the ground?
- What are the weather conditions?
- Am I wearing restrictive clothing/carrying equipment? (Backpack, winter overcoat, etc.)
- Are there any obstacles?
- Are there any objects usable as aids lying around?

What are the psychological factors?

- How alert am I?
- How good is my sense of perception?
- Am I able to note any specific characteristics about the opponent's actions? Can I detect when he is about to attack (dependent on knowledge and experience)?
- How far is my fighting spirit developed? How much am I in a position to overcome fear, and how strong is my will to win?
- How able am I to "depersonalize" the opponent so that I see him rationally as an enemy?

What are my technical capabilities?

- Which techniques have I mastered well with reliability?
- Have I any technical limitations?

What sort of condition am I in?

- Strength
- Stamina
- Mobility
- Speed
- Coordinative capability

How convinced am I of my fighting ability and myself?

- Belief in my self-sufficiency
- Anticipation of success
- Fully committed – the half-hearted is the loser!

Are complete fighting actions embedded in my techniques?

- Fighting actions consist of the following elements:
  - *Preparation:* correct distance and position for a particular technique or sequence of techniques and any disguised actions by feinting
  - *Execution,* carried out as follows:
    1 Individual direct attacks
    2 Resulting from a gap in the opponent's cover
    3 Part of a combination or series of combinations
    4 Feinting maneuver: By carrying out an incomplete technique, creating a gap in the opponent's cover that is then attacked with a full, main technique
    5 Series of techniques executed without breaking the rhythm
    6 Counter move (delayed, simultaneous or pre-emptive)
  - *Pushing through against the attack:*
    1 Moving away from my attacker at an angle (Note: Never dodge in the same direction from which you have attacked.)
    2 At the end of a movement/action, putting the opponent off balance (push or pull his clothing)
    3 Maintain control by holding or turning the opponent around, as well as being able to throw him

What is my aim?

- Am I in a situation of self-defense or a sporting bout?
  - *Self-defense:* I want to get out of the situation unhurt (and cause as little injury to the opponent as possible)
  - *Tournament bout:* I want to win the bout and, where possible, demonstrate good techniques

1.4.2   A Fighter's Visual Focus

The fighter can only assess a combat situation appropriately when his flow of information is un-interrupted. He receives this information from his body's *perceptive organs*. (By the term percep-tive organs, we mean the sensory organs, like the eyes, ears or skin, and the stimuli-processing regions in the brain.) For middle and long distance actions (kicking/punching) the visual organs mainly provide the "flow of information." Which stimuli the fighter processes in his mind, and how he perceives it, depends on his knowledge and experience. These two factors enable the fighter also to anticipate the opponent's actions and predict them.

At close distances (knee/elbow/throwing techniques and groundwork), the fighter gains his in-formation in a *tactile* form from his sense of balance. In this chapter, however, we would like to examine visual perception in long distance situations.

Firstly, we look at the physiological characteristics of vision and determine how the flow of infor-mation mentioned above is maintained. The peripheral field of vision is limited to 47° upward, 65° downward, 60° sideways and 110° peripheral (provided the head and eyes are *not* moved). This field of vision can be increased by moving the eyes, but also by moving the head and the whole body.

A beginner tends to move his eyes, but this action has a distinct disadvantage. Through the mo-vement of the eyes and the concentration placed on a new point of focus, the flow of informa-tion is interrupted for a split second (0.2 to 0.3 seconds). Because this is so quick, the fighter as-sumes that the flow of information is continuous. But the fact is that during this period, a gap exists and only the brain perpetuates the interrupted flow of information. A continuous flow of information flutters in front of us. If the opponent manages to use a technique in this time gap, he catches the fighter as if he were "cold." He would have had no possibility to perceive any in-formation about the intended technique. He was − so to speak − blind at the crucial moment.

For visual focus at long distance, we therefore recommend that you:

•   Keep your eyes constantly focused, i.e., so that your eyes focus on one point, rather than on different target points.

•   Look at the opponent's breastbone or just above it. This way you gain the best benefits from the use of your visual focus. Try it and see what works best for you

1.4.3   Resolving Problems in a Fight Situation

We list the problems that confront you again here:

1) Mental confrontation

Self-control (→ Adrenalin)

Control of opponent (→ Actions)

2) Make effective use of the transference of your opponent's strength

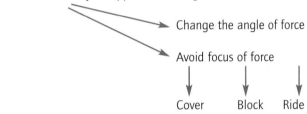

Change the angle of force

Avoid focus of force

↓	↓	↓
Cover	Block	Ride

3) Absorb the transference of opponent's strength

Change the angle of strike

Breathe out

Flex stomach muscles

Ride with the opponent's technique, i.e., sharpen the focus of the technique

4) Own optimal use of the transference of strength

In the following mind map, we show the conditions that lead to the optimal use of the transference of strength in your own techniques:

In order to neutralize the opponent's attack, the fighter normally uses a combination of numbers 2 and 3 as outlined above. That means he goes into the direction of attack, reactively tenses his stomach muscles, and redirects the attack past the sides of his own body.

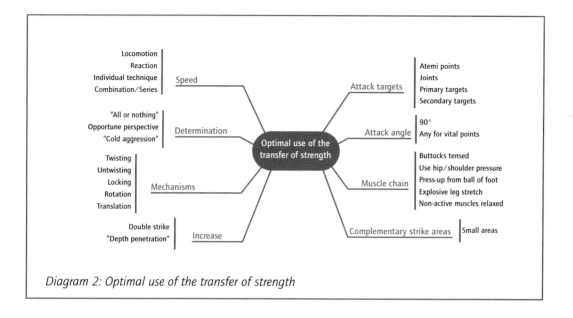

Diagram 2: Optimal use of the transfer of strength

1.4.4   The Three Elements of Fighting Action

In an idealized form, each combat action is made up of three elements:

1.   The preparation phase
2.   The execution phase
3.   Pushing through the attack

1. The preparation phase involves the Distance Rule I (i.e., the fighter shortens or lengthens the distance depending on the combination/series to be carried out). Linked to this is his *position* in relation to the opponent. The fighter conceals his own intentions, and "overfeeds" the enemy with false information, thus provoking disadvantageous reactions from the opponent by executing *feints* or *deceptive maneuvers*. These are also part of the preparatory phase.

By using "distance games," you can train your perception and assessment of appropriate distances. Here are some examples:

In the first game, you keep your distance from your partner. The latter attempts to shorten the distance between you. You prevent this by taking appropriate steps to maintain your distance.

This game can also be performed using techniques:

In this version, your partner is moving as economically as possible. He stays close to you and, at the same time, tries to escape your attack using minimal movement.

2. Once the fighter has created a situation that allows him to attack gaps created in the opponent's cover, he goes for these targets using specific, individual techniques/combinations/series.

3. Most fighters neglect the third part of ideal combat action: *Pushing through the attack or Distance Rule II*. If he does not include this part, then the fighter will be clearly and distinctly struck, even if it were previously a case in which he could successfully use his techniques. The instructor should therefore always ensure that the student correctly executes all three phases of combat actions during training.

1.4.5 Pushing Through the Attack – The Most Neglected Element in Fighting Action

As we have just explained, a complete combat action or chain of actions consists of three parts. Part 1 consists of preparatory footwork combined with feints. Part 2 includes individual techniques/combinations/series of techniques, while Part 3 is to push through the attack. In our experience, this last part in the chain of action does not receive the attention it deserves, neither in competition nor a real fight. Instructors and fighters simply ignore this action of pushing through against the attack. In a competition, this can lead to a fighter attacking successfully, but his opponent can still score a point. In a real situation (or even worse), the fighter "gives way" in a secure and controlled situation and ends up hurt.

Therefore, our urgent request to you as an instructor is to be sure you're your training includes <u>all</u> three parts of combat action. Do not focus exclusively on Parts 1 and 2.

In general, the fighter has two ways in which he can push through against an attack:

1. In a fight, the "channel of perception" forms a direct connection between the two opponents. Everything that happens in this "channel" (i.e., the direct connecting line), is fed into the perceptive senses and adequately "answered." How can the fighter use this knowledge? He starts an attack. He then moves at an angle out of the "channel of perception" into a direct line. This forces the opponent to re-orient himself in relation to distance and position. This creates a time gap in the opponent's actions for the fighter. Now he can use this for a fresh attack (see Chapter 1.4.2, "A Fighter's Visual Focus").

Note: Never dodge away in the same direction from which you have attacked

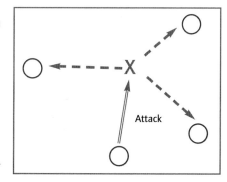

Diagram 3: Possible angles in which one can avoid the opponent

Examples:

After a mae-geri kick, the fighter places his attacked leg to one side and thus leaves the direct line of attack.

He meets the opponent's attempt at a counter by employing a technique from his new position.

Using a two-step turn, the fighter gets around partially behind the opponent's back.

2. As a second option for pushing through the attack, the fighter can use maneuvers that make a counter by his opponent impossible. Using the following examples, the fighter can disrupt the opponent's balance and thus prevent a counter-attack by:

- Controlling the opponent's elbow
- Using stop kicks
- Pushing the opponent away/disrupting his balance
- Using roundhouse sweeps against the opponent's feet
- Grabbing the opponent and shaking him (back and forth or up and down)
- Jostling the opponent

During sparring, the instructor and the fighter should *always* ensure that pushing through the attack is part of the combat action.

1.4.6   Ideal Distance, Long Distance, Short Distance and Handicap Distance in the Techniques

For each technique, there is an *ideal distance* that can maximize its impact. However, this distance is not always available or perhaps is only available for a fraction of a second in the fight. Therefore, students should first master the basic form of a technique and then test the full spectrum of that technique.

The *short distance* should be the shortest distance at which the technique still shows an effect. Accordingly, the *long distance* is the greatest range of a technique. In both forms, the fighter must be able to completely perform the technique (use of the entire muscle chain). In the *handicap distance*, he has to change the technique biomechanically, meaning parts of the muscle chain will be missing. An example of this is mawashi-geri that is executed using a stretched-out extension of the knee and without any action coming from the hip. Such a technique does not develop the same penetrating force as the versions above. The crucial question is, however: Which version of a technique is ineffective and needs to be replaced by another?

To summarize, the student should practice each technique in all four distances:
- Ideal
- Long
- Short and
- Handicap

The instructor should note that changeovers in the distances are done fluently. However, the students will practice being *more aware* of the differences.

1.4.7   An Outline of Groundwork

During a bout, a Karateka must sometimes continue to fight on the ground. He should not strive to execute the kind of skilful groundwork carried out by a Judoka as the time required for such training would be too long. The Karateka, however, has a big problem if he goes down onto the ground and is completely helpless.

The Karateka (in contrast to the Judoka) has two possible courses of action:
*   *He gets back up as quickly as possible into the standing position* (especially important in self-defense against multiple opponents!) OR
*   *He adopts a tactical position on the ground that allows him to hit and/or kick.*

The importance of groundwork springs to mind, especially in Mixed Martial Arts (MMA), and in All Round Fighting systems, such as the one practiced by Jon Bluming, 10th Dan Kyokushin Budo, and the various jiujitsu systems (specifically the Brazilian system). If the overall aim of training is to be capable at all distances then a Karateka has to come to terms with groundwork. Here, we consider the specific concepts and techniques that are necessary within the objectives listed above. The following rules should be internalized and practiced by the Karateka:

*   **When in the ground position, offer the smallest possible surface to the opponent**
    The fighter achieves this best by adopting the "embryo position." Here, his vulnerable parts are protected and he can hit, kick or grab his opponent.

*   **If the opponent is also on the ground, try getting alongside or behind him**
    This principle is similar to the standing position. If the fighter gets into the opponent's "blind spot" then he is clearly at an advantage!

*   **Strive to get into the position of the "diagonal arm"**
    Even if the fighter is lying underneath the attacker, he can still control one side of the opponent.

*   **One hand for controlling, one hand for striking!**
    Try to imagine you are a mountain climber! One of your hands is always in contact with the opponent! This way you can control him, feel him, know what he intends to do, disrupt him, confuse him and distract him, while the other hand can carry out offensive strikes, such as punches, eye gouging, hair-pulling, etc.

Try these few principles in groundwork and have a lot of fun!

These principles are demonstrated in the following examples:

Diagonal arm

The fighter pins the opponent's arm and upper body down ...

... and also pins the opponent's right ankle down using his left foot. In this way, the whole of the attacker's right side is pinned ...

... and he can be rolled over this pinned side.

1.5 Combinations Used in Fighting Action

1.5.1 Fighting Combinations Using a Modular System

When techniques are put together, they create fighting combinations. In contrast to the conventional view, these contain more building blocks than just the individual techniques. Additionally, we can also characterize combinations by the following features and categories:

* Distance
* Legwork (equivalent to step pattern)
* Attack angle (relative to the position of the opponent)
* Rhythm
* Different intensities of the individual techniques within the combination

Depending on the number of techniques in a combination, we differentiate between single and multiple content modules. As a reasonable limit, we use 3-5 techniques because the fighter will not be able to plan against the opponent's action if the combinations contain more techniques than this.

Combinations should generally meet two conditions:
1. The Karateka is able to use them *suitably in the fight*.
2. The Karateka can switch smoothly and seamlessly *from one technique to the next*.

We refer to this transition/switch as a phase merger (see the theory of motion by Meinel and Schnabel [2007]). This means that the final phase of the preceding technique merges with the initial phase of the following one. The bottom line for you as a fighter is as follows: If you build multiple content modules, do not simply string individual techniques together. Rather, treat the new combination as a whole unit, and practice it as such.

The modular system of combat combinations, described at the beginning of the chapter, will help you, as a Karate instructor, to structure your lessons. The combinations that consist of the same techniques can be practiced individually as per the listed characteristics or in varied manners.

How do you combine two techniques?
If you disregard the characteristics listed above, you have basically the following options:

1.	Arm – Arm	1) right-left or left-right
		2) with the same arm
2.	Leg – Leg	1) right-left or left-right
		2) with the same leg
3.	Arm – Leg	1) diagonal: right arm/left leg or left arm/right leg
		2) simultaneously: right arm/right leg or left arm/left leg
4.	Leg – Arm	1) diagonal
		2) simultaneously

For methodological reasons, we recommend you build up combinations in this order:

Arm – Arm	right-left or left-right
Arm – Leg	diagonal
Leg – Arm	diagonal
Leg – Leg	right-left or left-right
Arm – Arm	the same arm
Arm – Leg	simultaneously
Leg – Arm	simultaneously

A multiple module with three elements is created when you include individual techniques (single module). In modules of three elements, you can vary these according to step pattern, angle of attack, rhythm and intensity of the individual technique.

Make sure that in the fight combinations, no recurrence of motor skill systematizing slips in. In other words, don't always do the same move! Otherwise, later on, you will forget how to adapt to each actual fight situation.

When we look at the training methods in traditional Shotokan Karate, it occurs to us that the training objective is to achieve the perfect form. The Karatekas have to get as near as possible to a particular ideal model of the technique. For our purposes, in a fight, this is not enough!

For you, it will be crucial in a fight that you can use *variations* of techniques and combinations. This way, you will be able to adapt to rapidly changing situations and remain unpredictable. An example: Your special technique is ushiro-geri. Your opponent knows this. Nevertheless, you repeatedly hit him with it because you start the movements using different maneuvers, such as using variable step patterns, feints, different speeds, etc.

As a successful fighter, you must master several variations of the same technique.

Your *fighting capability* is always the ultimate aim in your training.
    (This is in contrast to the Kata training often practiced, where *precision in the form* is the top priority, meaning even your 100th repetition of a technique is done still as the best specific ideal model of a technique).

For your success in a fight, it is crucial that you:
* Develop strength to escape from *unfavorable positions* and
* Hit with *precision*.
Train both points.

1.5.2   How One Develops Useful Combinations or Series

Below, we show the principles by which you can build meaningful combinations/series. The term *combination* means a combination of two techniques, while a *series* consists of three or more techniques. Once again, if you build techniques into combinations or series, do not simply string them together. Rather, treat the combination/series as units with their own rules. You must also practice them as a unit, as well.

There are three basic ways in which you can execute the techniques in succession (despite whether they constitute punches, striking blows or kicks):

1.   You use techniques that involve maximum short muscle tension at the end of the strike *(kime)*. An example of this can be seen in Shotokan Karate with the *ikken-hissatsu principle* ("to kill with one stroke"). Behind this is the idea of solving a situation with a single technique.

2.   You use a number of techniques that are strung together but are rather unconnected. In most cases, fluid movement is lost when you do this (e.g., *piston hitting)*.

3.   If the final phase of your previous technique moves into the initial or pull-back phase of the next technique without interruption, then this is considered to be *flow-hitting*. This means that the flow of movement is uninterrupted at all points. How do you achieve this smooth transition? Tense and relax your body's longitudinal axis, then rotate it. Start the technique on a curved or straight trajectory that switches directly into a curved path. Doing this will allow you to achieve a constant flow of movement.

As an instructor, make sure that your students perform each technique of a combination/series *with the whole body* and not just with the arms or legs. You can judge the execution of the technique using the following criteria:

Precision: Is the fighter attacking the gap in the opponent's cover that was created by the previous technique with precision? It is a question of being only just a few centimeters off!

Force/speed: It is not possible to deliver a strike with 100% speed and 100% force at the same time. The ratio of the mix is the problem. This means that depending on the intention of a technique (preparation, final technique), the focus is either more on the speed or more on the force.

Flow of movement: Is there a break or momentary interruption between the various techniques in a combination/series? Does the fighter execute each technique with the whole of the body? Is it a question of phase merging, i.e., does the end phase of the previous technique follow "smoothly" into the pull-back phase of the following technique?

Trajectory: Does the fighter always execute his techniques with the same trajectory? Is the trajectory permanently bent or straight? Are there "breaks" in the transition between techniques? (If yes, please correct.)

Rhythm: Does the fighter accentuate the main techniques properly in the framework? Does he distribute them sensibly in time or space (important in delaying actions or interrupted rhythm)?

Each connection between techniques (i.e., in combinations and/or series), is created by joining an individual technique or two of them. We have chosen the term "module" because we are treating the techniques as building blocks in a larger overall context.

A combination of individual technique modules (single technique module = STM) is built as follows: You start the technique with the right arm and combine it with a left arm technique or leg technique.

A double technique module (DTM) is created as follows: You start two techniques by using the same limb. For example: Shita tsuki – Mawashi tsuki with the left arm. You have the possible following scenarios:

1. **STM + STM + STM**
Example: Oi-tsuki left + Gyaku-tsuki right + Mawashi-tsuki left

2. **STM + DTM**
Example: Oi-tsuki left + Shita tsuki right + Hiji-uchi right

3. **DTM + STM**
Example: Oi-tsuki left + Oi-tsuki left (= Double Jab) + Jodan-mawashi-geri right

4. **DTM + DTM**
Example: Mae-geri/Mawashi-geri, both techniques with right + Gyaku-tsuki/Hiji-uchi, both with the left

Scenario 1 suits a beginner best, because here he can rotate around the longitudinal axis of the body better and thereby strengthen his techniques. In order to make the basic concept of this clear to the student, he can also execute it in an exaggerated form.

At first, DTM combinations will be somewhat difficult for the student to manage. Here, after the first technique, he must execute a short counter rotation in order to be able to land a strike with the necessary force in the following technique. Therefore, students must first learn the proper mechanics of the DTMs before they connect them with STMs or/and DTMs. The possibilities available in putting together STMs can be represented in the form of a matrix.

Matrix I (Arm techniques): STM + STM
OT = Oi-tsuki
GT = Gyaku-tsuki
ST = Shita-tsuki
MT = Mawashi-tsuki
HU = Hiji-uchi

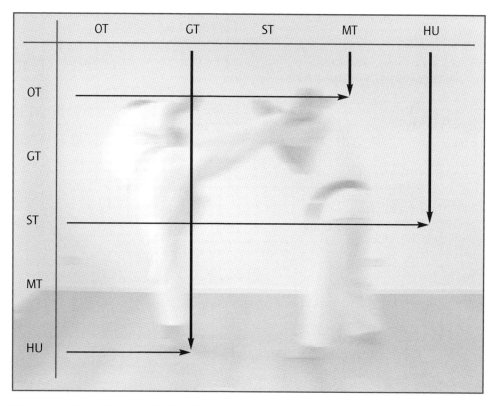

Diagram 4: Matrix I (Arm techniques)

Matrix II (Leg techniques) STM + STM
MG = Mae-geri
MAG = Mawashi-geri
YG = Yoko-geri
UG = Ushiro-geri
UMG = Ushiro-mawashi-geri
KOG = Kagato-otoshi-geri
HG = Hiza-geri

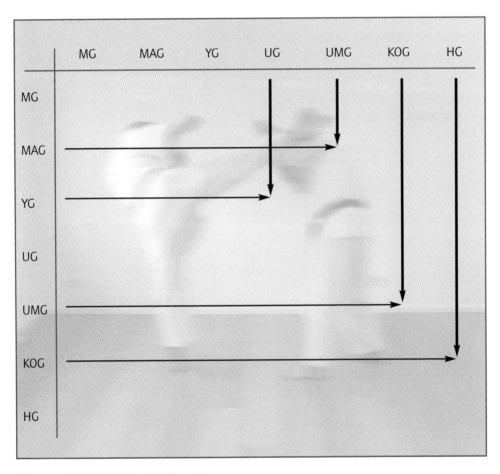

Diagram 5: Matrix II (Leg techniques)

When fighters combine arm and leg techniques, the best way to teach it is as a diagonal combination. The fighter, therefore, combines techniques using a pattern of right arm + left leg and vice versa. This way, he can make a smooth transition from one technique to the next. Moreover, doing it this way, he can also develop and optimize his strength.

When the fighter executes *combinations on the same side*, such as right arm-right leg, he can develop his strength mainly by moving his whole body in a line without turning around *(= translation)*. It is possible that he bends his hips, as well *(flexing the hip area)*. As a result, he kicks with his upper body leaning slightly backwards while at the same time bringing his fist back. Then he thrusts his body forward and delivers a punching technique.

In DTMs, you will find that it is much harder to develop force with two techniques. As an instructor, you have to make sure that a DTM is *always done as a full body movement*. In training, you must clearly state what the student should focus on. The development of long sequences of techniques (STM + DTM, DTM + STM, DTM + DTM) can only be achieved once the fighter can execute a DTM as a unit and can strike with the necessary development of force.

As examples, we show DTMs using the **arm** and **leg**.

Examples of Arm DTMs:

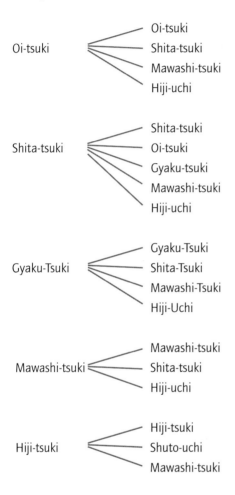

Oi-tsuki
- Oi-tsuki
- Shita-tsuki
- Mawashi-tsuki
- Hiji-uchi

Shita-tsuki
- Shita-tsuki
- Oi-tsuki
- Gyaku-tsuki
- Mawashi-tsuki
- Hiji-uchi

Gyaku-Tsuki
- Gyaku-Tsuki
- Shita-Tsuki
- Mawashi-Tsuki
- Hiji-Uchi

Mawashi-tsuki
- Mawashi-tsuki
- Shita-tsuki
- Hiji-uchi

Hiji-tsuki
- Hiji-tsuki
- Shuto-uchi
- Mawashi-tsuki

As you can already see, the first step in the DTM arm technique is the combination of a technique with another. This means that you shorten the pull-back for the first technique and bring the kinetic energy directly into the second technique.

For DTMs with the legs, we can differentiate between variations where *the foot is placed down* after the first technique and ones where *it is not placed down*.

Examples of Leg DTMs:

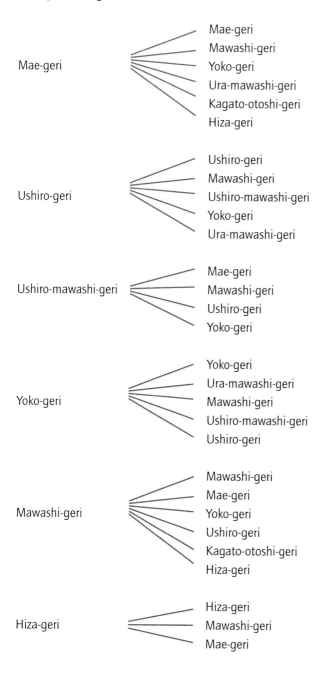

Mae-geri
- Mae-geri
- Mawashi-geri
- Yoko-geri
- Ura-mawashi-geri
- Kagato-otoshi-geri
- Hiza-geri

Ushiro-geri
- Ushiro-geri
- Mawashi-geri
- Ushiro-mawashi-geri
- Yoko-geri
- Ura-mawashi-geri

Ushiro-mawashi-geri
- Mae-geri
- Mawashi-geri
- Ushiro-geri
- Yoko-geri

Yoko-geri
- Yoko-geri
- Ura-mawashi-geri
- Mawashi-geri
- Ushiro-mawashi-geri
- Ushiro-geri

Mawashi-geri
- Mawashi-geri
- Mae-geri
- Yoko-geri
- Ushiro-geri
- Kagato-otoshi-geri
- Hiza-geri

Hiza-geri
- Hiza-geri
- Mawashi-geri
- Mae-geri

These examples give possible options that students can select from. The student is tasked to play through the options under the instructor's guidance until the combinations of techniques that emerge are the best ones for the individual. In order for the fighter to build up his own system, he must think through, try out and put in a lot of effort, all with the assistance of his instructor of course.

Use your brain, play with the possibilities, note which are the best and have fun with it!

1.5.3   Examples of Combinations in the Modular System

1.1	Jab – Cross	1.2	Jab – Jab
	Jab – Hook		Jab – Hook
	Jab – Uppercut		Jab – Uraken
	Cross – Hook		Hook – Hook

2.1	Mae-geri – Mae-geri	2.2	Mae-geri – Yoko-geri
	Mae-geri – Mawashi-geri		Mae-geri – Mae-geri
	Mawashi-geri – Ushiro-geri		Mae-geri – Mawashi-geri

3.1	Gyaku-tsuki – Mae-geri	3.2	Jab – Mae-geri
	Gyaku-tsuki – Mawashi-geri		Jab – Mawashi-geri
	Jab/uraken – Mae-geri		Cross – Mae-geri
	Jab/uraken – Mawashi-geri		Cross – Mawashi-geri
	Jab/uraken – Ushiro-geri		Cross – Ushiro-geri

4.1	Mae-geri – Gyaku-Tsuki	4.2	Uraken – Yoko-geri

1.6 The Timing of Defense-Counterattack Measures

In traditional Karate, the fighter carries out defense and counterattack, or counters one attack after the other. As a defender, he has a great disadvantage here because his attacking opponent has ample time to neutralize the block and avoid the counterattack.

The defending fighter should therefore execute defense and counterattack measures as rapidly as possible one after the other. Nevertheless, this does not address the problem that this approach is structurally slow.

We recommend that to start with you practice the classic sequence of defense and counterattack. Once the fighter has progressed, he can learn to execute defense and counterattacks using the same limb. Such action is already structurally faster. It calls for more of the fighter's skills, particularly in his coordination and adaptability.

Ultimately, the ideal training goal for the real fight or self-defense is that the fighter carries out defense and counterattack simultaneously. This method of meeting attacks demands a very high degree of coordination. The fighter may need to use different techniques simultaneously, each delivered with various intensities (e.g., soft defense and hard counter).

2 Full Contact Karate in Practice

2.1   The Basics of Its Usage/Application

2.1.1   The Starting Stance as a Basis for Defense and Attack

In Full Contact Karate, the fighter adopts a natural, relaxed stance. In order to allow your actions to be best used, an optimum fighting stance (on guard position) must possess the following requirements:

* Stability
* The ability to permit movement in all directions without having to make adjustments or delays
* Provide optimum cover against the opponent's attacks
* The ability to attack the opponent using all four limbs

Economy in movement and the ability to "explode" depend on the fighter moving well and being as relaxed as possible. This way the fighter also avoids getting tired too quickly.

The technicalities for the achievement of the optimum requirements could be as follows:

On-guard position with open or clenched fists

* The center of balance is directly over a point between the feet
* The hands are held at head height (the fists are either held open or lightly clenched)
* The elbows are held to protect the lower ribcage
* The feet are placed almost parallel with the toes pointing forward or the feet are placed slightly inward
* The fighter keeps moving because this gives him energy to start any defense or attack

Concentrate on the on-guard position and its usage in connection with your footwork and techniques. Make sure that it is done in a flowing, continuous movement.

Variation with clenched fists   Variation with open hands

2.1.2   Attack Angles/Strike Angles Against the Opponent

From a front perspective
Looking at the opponent from a front perspective, the aim is to create or build up the fighter's repertoire of techniques so that he is in a position to launch an attack from any direction.

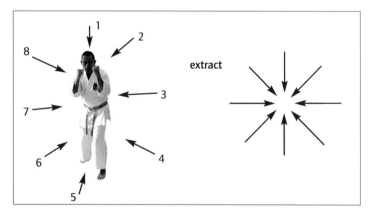

Diagram 6

In an ideal case, the fighter is in a position to vary the attack angle of an individual, specific technique. In this way, he gains the greatest possible variation availabile in a technique.

The three classic areas of attack – jodan, chudan and gedan – indicate the height of the attack but not the angle of attack. They do not also say anything about the optimum position relative to the target of the attack. When we analyze the techniques that have been passed on, we see that we can trace them back to the demands of a situation. The facts are shown here in an example in legwork:

Mae-geri is a technique executed in a straight line against an opponent who is attacking from the front. Yoko-geri and ushiro-geri are also techniques executed in a straight line against an attack coming from one side or behind. Mawashi-geri was developed from the necessity "to kick around the corner," so to speak (e.g., against an opponent who has good front cover).

The demands of the Okinawa style of Karate dictates that kicks should not be above hip height for two reasons:

- The requirements for one's own safety
- At an attack angle of approximately 90°, the maximum destructive effect can be achieved.

Such an ideal execution is less important if the fighter attacks an opponent's sensitive points. In these cases, the force need not be developed so much in order to make the attack effective.

Also, if we disregard the aspect of self-defense, a good fighter has to be versatile and, at the same time, unpredictable. Besides the *areas of attack*, his repertoire must also include techniques that can be used at *various attack angles*.

The technical profile of such a fighter – only considering the leg techniques – could look like this (the figures in front of the techniques correspond to the directions of attack in Diagram 6).

1, 2	Kagato-otoshi-geri
2, 3, 4	Mawashi-geri
5	Kinteki-geri (a form of snap-kicked mae-geri at the lower abdomen. An excellent method to practice the technique for the snap kick or the stretching movement of the knee and the pelvis upright is to push the hips forward. In comparison to other kicking techniques, this one is less complex and thus easier to learn. In all leg techniques, the biomechanical "hubs" are all the same. The kinteki-geri is therefore easier to learn because the position of the standing leg and thus the positioning of the pelvis in relation to the target determine the attack angle of the technique.)
6	Uchi-geri (executed as a low kick against the inside of the opponent's thigh, or a kick at the lower ribs with the shin bone.)
7	Gyaku-mawashi-geri
8	Ura-mawashi-geri/Kagato-otoshi-geri (outward)

An analysis like this is useful for the instructor in finding weak spots and allowing him to plan individual training for the students. The points of view listed above concern leg techniques with the right leg. You can conduct the same kind of analysis for left-legged techniques and arm techniques. For this, it is extremely important that the system of techniques that you pass on is adapted to the individual student and that the student is not pressed into accepting some sort of (allegedly) "ideal" hackneyed system of movement. The most important task that an instructor has is to seek the possibilities and limits of his students and to construct the training plan around these facts.

In summary, it is all about learning to punch, kick or strike effectively. The techniques passed on merely give an idea of how to develop the problem solving that the fighter eventually has to work out for himself.

2.1.3 How to Help Oneself Against Strikes and Kicks

- **Move in the direction of the strike.**
Often just a few centimeters are enough to lessen the effectiveness of a strike. The focus is held on causing the opponent to "overstretch" his technique, thus making it ineffective as much as possible.

- **Change the angle the attack comes in on.**
A technique achieves its maximum effectiveness when it strikes the target head-on 90°. When the blow lands more acutely, it loses more force.

Diagram 7

Examples:
Twist the pelvis around sideways to avoid a mae-geri kick.
Do a U-turn to avoid a punch at the temple.

- **Tense the stomach muscles reflexively.**

A technique aimed at the body that brings you down to the ground is one used when you have been caught in a relaxed posture! In training, we build in "dummy sessions" wherein the partner acts as the punching bag for the other. This kind of training develops a gradual increase of one's strength over time.

Tense the stomach muscles

- **Breathe out.**

Never get caught being struck while you are breathing in. The intercostal muscles (muscles between the ribs) may not be tensed when breathing in. Therefore, the rib cage is weak when breathing in and a rib can be broken if you are struck at that moment.

- **Learn how to handle pain.**

This is more or less a question of mental training. It is not the fact that you have been hit that stops you, but rather it is the importance of it that you measure against the whole event. An experienced fighter feels the same pain as a coward or someone inexperienced, but he doesn't attach the same importance to it. Getting used to being hit (for example, using the "dummy sessions" mentioned above) will help you learn how to handle pain.

2.1.4 The System of Controlling Techniques

Controlling techniques are those techniques that are designed to make the opponent's attacks ineffective and/or put him in a position of momentary helplessness (tactical moments [TM]). In the following sections, we give you insight into the important technical options.

2.1.4.1 Deflections

Principle:
Change the course of the straight-line or slightly bent trajectory of an incoming attack technique so that it glides past your body.

Techniques:
- Shotei-uke, or better still shotei-barai
- Gedan-barai with shotei or the soft inside of the lower arm (General rule: Use the soft parts of your body as a defense against hard strikes by your opponent and vice versa)
- Double gedan-barai – the deflection is done by executing two overlapping circular movements
- Shotei-barai with jodan-uke against jodan-mawashi-geri

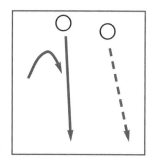

Diagram 8

Deflecting a mae-geri   Controlling the elbows

2.1.4.2 Blocks

Principle:
"Cut inside" against a curved attack trajectory. This interrupts or deflects the attack.

Techniques:
- Jodan-uke using the lower arm or shuto
- Juji-uke (Double block)
- Sune-uke (Using the shin bone to defend inward and outward)
- Sune/Kote-uke (combined blocking movement to protect the whole side being attacked)

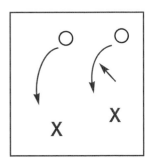

Diagram 9

2.1.4.3   Checks

Principle:
The opponent is put off balance momentarily; or alternatively, by contacting certain points on the opponent's body, he is prevented from continuing the attack. This then opens the possibility of conducting a counterattack.

Techniques:
- All forms of kuzushi (= loss of balance)
- Pushing away (near the shoulder or hip joint)
- Pulling opponent toward you sharply, and striking
- Sweeping movements: (Illustrated examples follow in a later chapter)
  - Uchi-ashi-barai
  - Soto-ashi-barai
  - Kuchiki-taochi
- Ramming your body into the opponent ("0-Distance")
- Oscillating movements ("rhythm-of-three")
  - Push away – Pull toward – Push away
  - Pull toward – Push away – Pull toward
  - Up and down
  - Sideways movements
- Pressing the elbow against the body → Part immobilization
- Turn the opponent's body (by using the shoulder joint)
- Positioning oneself to one side or behind the opponent

2.1.4.4   Grasping

Principle:
Grasp the head and/or elbows, upper arm between the shoulder and the elbow. This allows you to exercise control for longer than the "checks".

Techniques:
- Controlling the head
  - Single-handed

Grab parts of the clothing (as in Judo)

Stop kick and loss of balance

Pulling the opponent into a follow-up technique

Hiji-uchi

Finishing off with a hiza-geri

- Two-handed
  - Clinch.

One hand clasps the ball of the thumb of the other hand. The hands are lying at the back of the opponent's head. The elbows are pressed inward. This way the back of the opponent's head can be lowered down onto your own shoulder.

Grab hold of your own wrist, place your hand on the back of the opponent's head and lower his head down onto your shoulder.

- Both hands on one side of the head

- On the top of the head and neck

- Controlling the elbows
  - Diagonally downward
  - Diagonally upward

- Mawashi-uke (Elbow-Neck control + turn)
  For clarity, we only show the start of the grip here. We cover the typical Ashihara technique in more detail in Chapter 2.2.6.10 "Mawashi-uke."

2.1.5   Throwing Techniques in Full Contact Karate

Contrary to Judo, throws have no particular decisive function in Full Contact Karate. Rather, they serve to give one the opportunity to create a fight-winning technique (otoshi techniques) or to simply "take the wind out of the opponent's sails." Even if you do not have success with a throw, at least you have moved your opponent off-balance. As a result, you now have an opportunity to follow-up with a hiza-geri or hiji-uchi, etc.

In our opinion, the following throwing techniques should be learned. These almost cover the full spectrum of the various directions for throwing.

2.1.5.1   Throwing Forward/Diagonally Forward

*   Koshi-guruma/Harai-goshi
*   Kubi-nage/Tai-otoshi
*   Seoi-nage

Starting with a low kick

Start of a seoi-nage throw

Throw

- Makikomi-Nage (as shown in Chapter 2.2.6.10 "Mawashi-uke")
  - Follow-up from mawashi-uke
  - Grabbing the opponent's leg
- Uchi-Ashi-Barai

The opponent is grabbed hold of diagonally

Lunge step to the side and lower the center of balance

Start the sweeping movement. Note: The center of balance is kept low

Whoops! The opponent has just slipped on a banana skin (Actually the idea behind the sweep!)

2.1.5.2 Throwing Backward/Diagonally Backward

• O-soto-gari

From a clinch situation ...

... bring the opponent off-balance with a low kick

Starting an o-soto-gari. Control the opponent's head

Throw

Control (diagonal arm)

Finale – Cheerio!

- O-uchi-gari
  - From a mawashi-uke
  - Grab hold of the opponent's leg
  - Ko-uchi-gari
  - Ko-soto-gari
  - Ashi-barai
  - Morote-gari
  - Kata-ashi-dori/Kuchiki-taoshi

(We refrain from going into the details of each of the throws, but refer those interested readers to the excellent literature on Judo.)

These throws should always be practiced and internalized as punching or kicking combinations so that, in a fight, you are able to transfer fluidly and smoothly from one technique into the next.

2.1.6   Controlling the Opponent on the Ground

The fight is not yet finished just because the opponent has been put to the ground. He won't simply lie there and clap. If you want to apply a fight-winning technique, you have to control him on the ground.

Protect your lower abdomen by placing your knee on the opponent's ribs or into his armpit, while at the same time controlling his arm. This way he no longer has the ability to deliver a punch or a kick. If you use a controlling technique incorrectly, the opponent can still fight on while on the ground (see Illustration 5 on Page 58).

2.1.7   Biomechanics for the Karateka – Without Mathematics

For fighters who practice Full Contact Karate and instructors who teach it, a basic knowledge of biomechanics is absolutely essential.

This understanding supports the learning process. By using a scientific approach to tackle the subject, as an instructor you are in a position to explain why and how the students should execute a technique. Your students learn techniques based on biomechanics. Their training in Karate movements is more than just pure imitation with reference to a foolish tradition. A mae-geri can be measured by a scientifically proven standard, irrespective of whether it comes from the Chinese, Korean or Japanese style. For this, we do not need any mathematical formulae. In the following sections, we introduce several principles by which the students can analyze their techniques.

2.1.7.1   The Principle of the Acceleration Path

This principle is about the length of the acceleration path and its geometric course.

For example: It is better to deliver a hiza-geri knee kick using the rear standing leg because the path of acceleration is longer. The fighter can get into a position by using preparatory legwork (kosa-ho) so that he is at an optimum distance to execute a particular technique.

The geometric course should be straight or fully curved

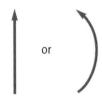

or

In practice, most of the leg techniques are executed using the same initial movement.

2.1.7.2   The Principle of the Tendencies in the Acceleration Phase

The quality of *explosiveness* is essential in Full Contact Karate. The important part of the acceleration phase is *at the beginning of the movement*. If the movement is too slow then the opponent can react. Also, the fighter has to slow down the technique in the final phase in order to prevent his joints from overstretching. The fighter can practice explosiveness as follows:

- By emphasizing the start of the movement
- By limiting his area of movement
- By executing a partial movement of his kinematic chain (e.g., making just a movement of the hips)

(Explanation: As an example, let us explain the kinematic chain in a *gyaku-tsuki*. The technique is started by pushing off from *the balls of the rear feet*. The leg is stretched out. The hips are turned inward. The transmission of force comes from the *shoulders*. Finally, the force is directed further through the *stretched arm* down to the *striking surface of the knuckles of the fist.*)

2.1.7.3   The Principle of Power in the Beginning Phase

When a fighter starts an action with a countermovement and then brings the movement imme-diately into the opposite direction, this develops a greater force than one done from a neutral position. The countermovement at the beginning brings the working muscles under tension by lengthening (optimally 120% of the neutral length) them so that the elasticity stored in the energy is brought into play. This, however, must be followed immediately by movement into the opposite direction. The fighter can "mask" the countermovement using a feint. For example, in a snap kick, the heel is brought up to the bottom and then immediately executes the kick.

2.1.7.4   The Principle of Coordinating Impetus Elements

All your movements in Full Contact Karate should be executed as whole movements of the body. This can be combined as follows:

*   *Translation* (you move the center of balance of your body in a particular direction in a straight line) and
*   *Rotation* (you turn your body or parts of your body about an axis, e.g., wind up/twist or unwind/untwist)

In practice, you do not develop maximum penetrating force by only striking with the arm or kicking with the leg. It is better to do as follows: Turn your torso by pushing off from your feet; then stop abruptly and translate the rotation of the body into the stretching of the arm or leg.

Partial impulses can also be coordinated into series when one technique transfers into another.

2.1.7.5   The Principle of Countermovement

The basis of this principle is the Newton's third law: action = reaction. Expressed simply, this means that a certain movement needs a countermovement in order to maintain the balance and to be able to develop a greater force. Examples:

*   The counter-rotation of the shoulder in a mawashi-geri when the axis of the hips moves in the direction of the kick in order to give it force
*   Pulling back the hand (that is not being used to strike with) to the chin or in kihon, to the armpit or hips (depending on the style)
*   Dropping the center of balance of the body when kicking by slightly lifting the standing leg during the initial movement of the kicking leg

2.1.7.6   The Principle of Maintaining Impetus

You can observe this principle when executing an ushiro-mawashi-geri. The idea is simple: Keep the kicking leg in the axis of rotation as long as possible in order to achieve a high rotation speed. You push your leg out only shortly before the finish.

If you execute the kick with a stretched leg from the beginning, you will only reach a relatively slow rotation speed.

2.1.7.7   The Principle of Reducing the Target Area

Examples of this principle can be seen by looking at the surface area hit by the knuckles of the fist, the tip of the elbow and nukite (a stab with the fingers).
       The smaller the surface area of the attacking limb, the greater the impact of the technique (inverse proportionality).

All Karate techniques can be explained and discussed under the aspect of this principle. If the student knows about this, he can build up his knowledge about movement structures and affinities. This will help him to improve and adapt the model techniques to the individual circumstances of his body.

2.2   Training

2.2.1   Motives for Karate Training

Any student who joins a Karate group has his own personal reasons, and his idea of what Karate is has been influenced by the media and other influences. However, motives change over time. For the moment, let us take a closer look at "the initial spark" that set you off. Motives can usually not be seen as a pure, single form. Rather, there are several overlapping motives in the individual's mind. They form a "complexity of motives."

Here, we list some categories and this gives us insight into the range of possible motives:

•   Self-defense
The desire to be able to defend oneself is, for many, at the top of the list of possible motives for taking up Karate training.

However, almost always the beginner is subject to misconceptions regarding the nature of Karate training. Often, he had no previous idea of what is trained or how. In time, the student usually replaces this motive with others.

- **Self-image/Self-confidence**

Karate can help build a positive self-image and a healthy measure of self-confidence. Practicing a martial art like Karate is especially suited for women.

- **Wellness/Health**

Karate training can be viewed as a counterbalance to the unnatural and sedentary way of life found in industrialized society.

- **Fitness**

Related to the previous motive, Karate is seen primarily as an "all-round workshop."

- **Risk/Adventure/Excitement**

Students are looking for the "adrenaline rush" of the challenge, e.g., such as tournaments. They want to experience the feeling of their own strength.

- **Progress/Competence/Knowledge**

The student wants to master a complex philosophical and technical system as a way of self-expression.

- **Communication/Community**

The dojo "community," with its clear structure, is designed in an ideal case to give a life-long opportunity for people to train and grow together. In the ever-increasingly complex and obscure structure of everyday life, the dojo community fosters a group of like-minded people who are committed to the same pursuit.

- **Exotic/Japanese traditions**

Relatively new styles, such Ashihara Karate or Kyokushinkai Karate are also deeply rooted in Japanese tradition. As a technically open system, Ashihara Karate also takes techniques from other systems and integrates them into its own. The philosophical and social superstructure is, however, geared strictly to Japanese ideals. In an increasingly detached era in time, such factors as strict discipline, hierarchical and general values (those that are lost in everyday life today) are fascinating.

In summary, Ashihara Full Contact Karate has many benefits, and thus is able to satisfy different needs. Over time, the individual may well change the weight and combination of his motives. By virtue of the complexity of Ashihara Karate or similar styles, no problems will result from this.

2.2.2   Relationship Between Instructor and Student

In martial arts, the central role model for the students is the sensei. Originally, this special relationship stems from a social environment that is heavily characterized by the Zen Buddhist and Confucian influences. In these instances, the instructor is not just a mentor and role model in the field of martial arts, but rather, the role model concept applies to almost all areas of life. In Western society, we do not find such a role model concept as this.

In Ashihara Full Contact Karate, the instructors achieve their legitimacy and authority by virtue of their superior knowledge and their role as primus inter pares (i.e., first among equals). Their instructions are justified by their experience and insight into the need to prevent potential dangers. The teaching takes place in a friendly but disciplined atmosphere. Their authority is limited to that which they teach. Outside of the training, they are not "budo-gods" who want to be admired by their students. A good instructor helps his students to achieve their limits and be aware of their potential. In this manner, they can build up self-respect and self-confidence without being arrogant toward those who may not be as talented.

A good instructor shares his knowledge with his students and tries to make them better Karatekas, like himself. He feels responsible for their progress and is keen to teach people, and not turn them into obedient robots. At best, a good instructor fulfills an important function for his students by enriching their lives.

2.2.3   Developing the Correct Approach

Hard training always leads to effects in areas of life that do not have anything particular to do with the actual training itself. A student who practices Karate seriously is confronted with a concept that impacts all areas of life. In the best case, the martial art represents a way of coping with his life. The student is confronted with frustration, pain and the feeling of not being able to reach his ability, etc. Practicing Karate is a lifelong activity, not a short-term affair. With the determination of never giving up and having patience that results from the perspective of lifelong learning, students will inevitably be successful.

Remember: The only standard that really matters is your personal progress!

Other standards that are set for you externally are unimportant because they do not take your personal requirements into account.

What is the primary objective in Full Contact Karate? It is not all about doing a perfect technique or being a good fighter. Rather, it is the process itself of pursuing goals like these and being aware that this process is a never-ending journey. The "perfect product" is of secondary importance and is perhaps a by-product of your participation.

Randall Hassell (1985), a highly qualified Karate instructor, describes purpose as follows:

> The purpose of budo is not to gain a wide knowledge for the purpose of fighting. Rather, the purpose of budo is to gain a very, very deep knowledge of one's art in order to perfect one's character and see more clearly and deeply into the nature of one's existence.

In its origins, Karate was a matter of life and death. Therefore, it is now, when taken seriously, more than a game and exceeds the range of sport. The very nature of Karate demands that its study is taken seriously.

For example, in the full contact type of Ashihara Karate, the student is soon confronted with having to deal with pain. He must decide whether to abandon or continue his career in Karate. The dojo etiquette states that he has only the choice of either accepting the painful aspects of the exercises openly or giving up. During the process of becoming a would-be Karateka, the student learns to internalize these visible impressions. He still feels the pain, but he measures it with another importance than at the beginning. By feeling his own pain, the student develops empathy for the pain of others and interdependently feels a sense of responsibility for his partner. Alongside the formal discipline of dojo etiquette, an internal discipline grows that allows advanced students (kohai) to reach their limits, progress beyond these limitations, but not break them. In this way, we can interpret Ashihara Karate and all Full Contact Karate styles as a way of life that is diametrically opposed to a pure consumer mentality.

Another quote by Hassell (1985):
> I was always taught the "hard way" was the only way to learn Karate. In the Buddhist tradition, the Japanese are taught there are two ways to go through life. One is the way of jiriki (the way of self-denial and self-reliance). My teacher explained jiriki is the way of walking along the road, facing and overcoming all obstacles. Tariki, he said, is like riding through life in a limousine with a chauffeur at the wheel. He said most people go through life in the tariki manner, and they never gain real strength or deep insight into themselves. When he spoke of jiriki as a way in Karate, he called it nangyo-do (the way of hardship). If you take the easy way, he warned, you cannot learn Karate-Do.

For the beginner, Karate styles like Ashihara Karate appear outwardly to be very aggressive martial arts. Almost automatically, one compares the "aggressive actions" with a corresponding aggressive attitude. In time, the student learns, however, that this comparison is wrong. Aggressiveness hinders the clear perception and analysis of a combat situation and is therefore counterproductive.

The mark of a real fighter and Karateka is patience, persistence and thoughtfulness. Anger, fear and hatred lead to pain and defeat. Hence, fighting in the terms of a controlled, deliberate confrontation and of aggression are mutually exclusive of one another.

In the course of time, the student often has a different problem. He has the feeling of treading on the spot and not moving forward. Subjectively, he makes no progress in executing the techniques. Such a flat phase is quite normal. The body processes and consolidates the training input from the previous periods before the whole system can rise to a higher level. Many beginners, and unfortunately advanced students, give up training during this flat phase purely out of frustration. They think that performance improves linearly and steadily. They do not understand that, in reality, progress in performance is made in steps. A good instructor registers such frustrations and catches them before it is too late. He teaches the students that these flat phases all belong to the learning process. Progress is made from phase to phase. Once the student has understood this, it will help him continue training, even if he has the feeling that he is making no progress.

Ultimately, therefore, the term "Master" does not mean that someone has achieved the execution of a perfect technique, or in other words has reached "the end of the path." Rather, he has merely picked his way through obstacles, opposition and self-doubt.

He has gained a mental attitude that allows him to continue and develop a personal goal for any age he might be. A real master only measures his personal progress by continually learning, training and teaching his students without thinking about his personal shortcomings and weaknesses, and because of this he always remains modest. Being a Budoka means to be a student of the martial arts for his entire life, regardless of whether he is a beginner, *sensei*, or even *shihan* or *hanshi*.

2.2.4   Forms of Layout for Organizing Instruction

For the smooth operation of a Karate lesson, especially when the hall is small and the number of students large, the instructor can draw upon proven forms of organization. The traditional form of grouping into a square bears the disadvantage that, with a large number of students, the instructor's demonstration is not visible to all. As a rule of thumb and depending upon the upcoming task, the form to be chosen is one that makes it possible for all to have an unobstructed field of vision and ability to communicate. In the following examples, we cover various layout forms.

Symbol: (L)   = instructor

        ∧   = student, the head of the symbol indicates the direction of view.

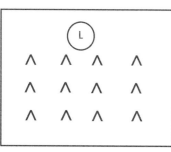

2.2.4.1   Square

Traditional layout form used for the greeting at the beginning and end of the session. Has a limitation for use with demonstrations.

Diagram 10

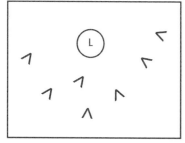

2.2.4.2   Free – No Laid Down Layout

Each student can see the instructor. Everyone is freely spread around the room for gymnastics and exercises not requiring control.

Diagram 11

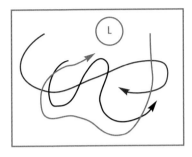

2.2.4.3 Free Movement Around the Room

For running games, etc.

Diagram 12

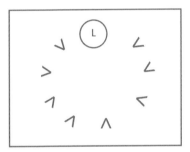

2.2.4.4 Circle

For gymnastics, shadow boxing, basic techniques. Has a motivating effect because everybody can see. Instructor can be part of the circle or take a position inside or outside, depending on what and where he wants to direct the focus of his attention.

Diagram 13

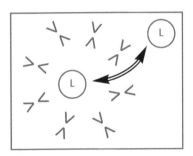

2.2.4.5 Double Circle

Good for partner exercises with a large number of students. To change partners, the outer or inner circle rotates. The instructor is positioned inside or outside the circle.

Diagram 14

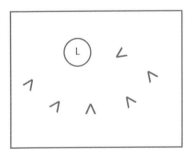

2.2.4.6 Half-circle

Very good for technique demonstrations because every student can see the instructor.

Diagram 15

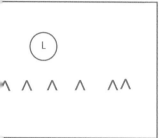

2.2.4.7   Line-up

Good form for any training content; limited by number of students.

Diagram 16

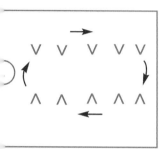

2.2.4.8   Double Line-up

Suitable for all partner exercises. Change of partners occurs by rotating clockwise or counterclockwise.

Diagram 17

2.2.5   Training Methods

2.2.5.1   Warm-up Phase/Cool-down Phase

In this short chapter, we explain reasons for and the effects of the warm-up or cool-down phases.

Theory and Background of the Warm-up Phase

Physiological objectives and effects:
- Increases the temperature of the muscles and the body's core (Optimum: 101 to 103° F). The muscles need about five minutes to warm up, the body core approximately 30 minutes. This is not to say that the warm-up phase must be 30 minutes long. Rather, it depends more on what movements will be trained afterward
- Increases metabolic rate
- The metabolic rate increases by about 13% per degree rise in temperature
- The efficiency of the nervous system is increased
- Perception and reaction speed increase. In a warmed-up status, the muscle spindles (measured as the amount of stretch and speed of change in length of the muscle) allow all movements to be performed with better coordination

- Speed of muscle contraction is increased.
- Prevention against injury by:
  - Enlargement of the cartilage in the joint
  - Increase in the elasticity and plasticity of the connective tissue
  - Decrease in the stiffness of the muscles. They become more supple and relaxed. This is especially important for the other muscles involved in a movement. (Example: Mae-geri. The flexor muscle in the leg slows down the straight line movement of the kick. If it has too much tonicity and cannot be relaxed, the mae-geri cannot be executed optimally)
  - Decrease in joint loading
- The initial oxygen deficit is reduced by:
  - An economical way to breathe (breathing deeply, abdominal breathing)
  - Less lactate accumulation in the blood. (Start slowly and then increase rather than a massive blast at the beginning)
  - Increased oxygen uptake. It is possible to guarantee a larger oxygen intake over a longer period during exercise training or competition
- Revising Karate-specific movement patterns. You carry out controlled techniques slowly and accentuated

Psychological aims and effects:
- Increase in motivation and familiarity with the burden of training and/or competition
- Regulating the level of arousal
- Overexcited fighters experience a normal level of arousal. Fighters who remain passive can increase their level of arousal to the amount necessary
- Mental support by employing a familiar warm-up routine
- Emotional stimulation of the fighting spirit

Basic Structure of the Warm-up Phase in Training

1. General warm-up by:
   - Skipping
   - Running games
   - Going through standard situations in a fight in order to improve rhythm and movement patterns
   - Using musical accompaniment, such as Capoeira does, in order to increase motivation and to forget the effort
2. Specific warm-up by:
   - 1-3 rounds of shadow boxing with predetermined techniques or free actions depending on the training goal and the degree of advanced level of the students
   - Active stretching for high kicks (controlled, execution of the trajectory)

3. Individual warm-up by:
    *   Stretching and working through the individual weak points. After a time, good instruc-
        tors recognize these points in their students and give them feedback.
4. Moving on to regular training with tonicity (increasing tension) of the trunk muscles. 5-10
    repetitions for each muscle group are sufficient.

We recommend that you schedule 10-30 minutes for the warm-up phase. The length is ultimately dependent upon what topic and tasks are planned for the training session. Standardized,
ritual warm-up exercises that always take the same form make no sense!

Cool-down Phase

In a way, the cool-down phase is a mirror image of the warm-up phase. The point here is that
you "drain off" the metabolic processes increased by the training.

Effects:
*   Relaxation of the muscles
*   Accelerated breakdown of the acid products of metabolism
*   Less time is required for regeneration
*   Generally, efficiency is increased, and you are quickly back into shape!

Methods of doing cool downs:
*   Relaxed trotting
*   Stretching
*   Massage
*   Slow versions of techniques and combinations

2.2.5.2   Aspects of Instructor Demonstrations

As an instructor, you demonstrate each arm, leg and control technique with the following
aspects:

1.   Analysis – "hub" of the technique
You teach the reason why the technique is effective, i.e., what the core or main points are. These
points have to be covered by the instructor during the demonstration.

2.   Demonstration without a partner
Using the demonstration, you can concentrate on how the theoretical principles of body
mechanics are implemented.

3. **Demonstration with a partner**
Here, you highlight the main target points on the body of the partner.

4. **Demonstration with punch-gloves/punching bag**
Here, you put the focus on the development of power in the technique.

5. **Demonstrating the technique in a combat situation**
By using the technique in a combat situation, you can complete or round off the student's understanding of a technique.

By using these five aspects in demonstrating the techniques, you create the framework from which your students can learn many facets of their own techniques.

In the next step, you cover how a fighter should use the technique (as seen from the opponent's point of view) in a fight (to lure, deflect, neutralize).

In the third step, you demonstrate the way to deal with the complexities of a single technique. You show the preparatory actions (footwork, feints) and the possibilities of combining them with other techniques (the main ones), as well as making the attack. Here, you also incorporate tactical considerations and eventually drills.

With this sequence of steps, you now have a possible guideline on how to embed an individual technique into a more complex situation.

2.2.5.3 Tips for the Demonstration of Techniques in Front of the Students

Because everyone learns in different ways, as an instructor you must use as many "input channels" as possible to impart information to your students during your demonstrations. The following procedure has been proven in practice:
*   You demonstrate the technique 2-3 times from different perspectives and at realistic speeds.
*   You show the main phases of the technique while *briefly* explaining and describing it. You stress here the important parts of the movement.
*   After that, you show the technique 2-3 times with *slow* movements. At the same time, you choose words or slogans for the more important details.
*   You demonstrate the technique again at a realistic speed. Keep this phase short.

Generally, we recommend that if your students are young, you emphasize the visual part and carry out the part with explanations in appropriate language for their age.
*   After the demonstrations, the students practice for a short time to collect together their *first experiences of the movement* for the new technique and the *inherent difficulties* with it.

- After the introductory phase, show the technique once again, but this time shorter than at the start.
- Your students' basic idea of a movement will be enriched by these first movement experiences.
- Now let the students exercise for a longer period.
  IMPORTANT: Errors must be immediately corrected!

2.2.5.4   Correcting Mistakes and Instructor Feedback

In principle, beginners especially need their errors corrected and your feedback provided as an instructor. Once errors creep in, relearning is only done with great difficulty! ("Learning is easier than relearning!")

Therefore, as an instructor, use the following key phrases:
- Correct an error *as soon as possible.*
- Correct an error *individually.*
- Correct only *one error at a time.*
- Correct the *most basic error at the start.*
- Build a *control mechanism* for the students, such as orientation points, lines on the ground, and the like from which the students can get feedback.
- Educate your students to *help and correct each other.*
- Give your students *enough time* to cope with their mistakes and correct them.
- *Encourage* your students and praise them.

In this way, you will have much joy instructing.

2.2.5.5   Methodically Building up the Teaching of the Techniques

In the classic styles of Karate, the instructor teaches the techniques (mainly) without any context. The techniques stand virtually by themselves, i.e., they apply only to the individual technique themselves. The instructor does not explain and show how, where and when the techniques can be applied. In his demonstration, he covers no preparatory or follow-up actions. He does not develop a larger understanding whereby the students can recognize which situations and contexts the techniques can be meaningful and effective.

This is what we authors call an "educational gap." The student learns the technique from its basic form right up through to its total perfection. However, it is only later in practice that he learns (if at all) in what variations he can or should use the technique and in which combat situations.

If the student practices techniques for the Kata exercises, he should strive for accuracy that can be described as the *"precision form."* In other words, even the 100th repetition does not differ (or only minimally) from the first. The precision that is required in combat, however, differs very much. It can be best described as *"target precision,"* i.e., the basic techniques are modified and adapted to the particular configuration and requirements.

In the following examples, we suggest an order for teaching the techniques. This is not a "score check" in the sense that the student has to master point 1 before he can move on to point 2. With our model, we try to cover the factors that will train the students. These factors are key to ensuring that the student is ultimately successful in his fight.

As an instructor, you can adopt the following methodology: You can summarize individual points and stress particular aspects. You decide which to choose, depending on how much this is required for special or training groups or individual students.

Our list includes the points as key words (we deal with these in detail elsewhere in this book). Duplication and overlaps cannot inevitably be ruled out, but they serve to highlight the issues addressed.

1. **Learning the traditional form**

2. **Form + Impact = firm, predetermined distance**

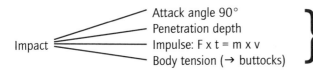

Impact
- Attack angle 90°
- Penetration depth
- Impulse: F x t = m x v
- Body tension (→ buttocks)

}
- Makiwara
- Coaching mitt
- Punching bag

3. **Development of power in the short and long form of a technique**

4. **Integrating basic step patterns**
    - Tsugi-ashi
    - Ayumi-ashi
    - Kosa-ho/Half-Step
    - Tai-sabaki
    - Composite pattern

5. **Partner exercises → Practicing judging distances**
    - Using the **"sun dome" principle (3cm)**
      - Principle of angles

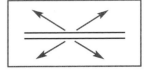

- Prevention of injury
- Special features: The limbs have extension possibilities
- Positioning
  - Principle of angles ("Don't retreat in the direction of an incoming attack")

  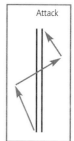

  - Zig-zag principle as a wider form of the principle of angles

  - Horizontal
  - Vertical
  - Zanshin + break away (as part of the principle of angles)
- Rhythm
  - Calculable, regular
- Structure Defense – Counterattack
  - Successive
  - Timed structure compressed by defensive counterattack using the same limb (in fencing "Battuta")
  - Simultaneous defense and counterattack

6. **Combinations**
   - Sequence of initiating combinations

     - Arm – Arm
     - Arm – Leg
     - Leg – Arm
     - Leg – Leg

     }
     - Phenomenon of the phase merger
     - The combination is more than just executing techniques successively
     - Translation + Rotation = Tension + Relaxation

7. **Combinations + Distance work + Development of Power**
   - Makiwara
   - Arm punching kit
   - Punching bag
   - Partner ⟶ stationary
                 ⟶ moving

8. **Fighting with a partner**
   - Watch for completeness:
   A   Distance Rule I   + feint (watch angle principle)
                                 + disruptive action (putting off balance)
   B   Single technique/combination/series
   C   Distance Rule II (pushing through the attack by avoidance)

- Opportunities for partner collaboration
- Acting cooperatively
- Slightly demanding actions
- Predetermined disruptive actions integrated
- Fight → free actions

9. **Sparring**
   - With tactical tasks 1: 1, 2: 1, 1: 1: 1 – for a single occasion
   - Concealment of the distance rule by feinting
   - Intended secondary action → opponent moves to the optimal distance
   - Exercise forms:
     - Ippon-kumite
     - Increase pressure on timing through line-up

   - In the circle (happo-kumite)

Diagram 18

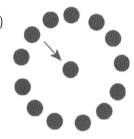

   - In a line

Diagram 19

   - 2:1

Diagram 20

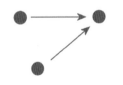

   - 3:1

Diagram 21

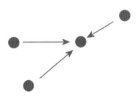

10. Handicap sparring
    - Only arms, legs
    - Only left/right
    - Target
    - Prognostic – only the technique that proved to be a point winner before counts
    - Training for the only option
    - Pressured timing (e.g., "Only 20 seconds allowed for scoring!" or similar)
    - Sparring after exertion: push-ups, squats and similar
    - Arm, leg sparring on one leg
    - On the knees (on a mat)
    - Uphill, downhill
    - In sand
    - In water

11. Adjusting to opponents' strikes and neutralizing them
    - Abdominal muscle tension
    - Change in incidence angle of attack from normal to an acute angle
    - Breathing technique: Only being hit during the exhalation phase
    - Kyushu:
        - Absorbing the effect of the opponent's impact
        - Dissipation of focus of the technique by going along with the technique
    - Moving in on the opponent's technique in the initial stage so that the technique is not allowed to develop → *Note: Precise timing is of importance for survival!*

2.2.5.6   The Instructor's Methods Matrix

The following matrix serves as an instructor's planning tool. You start with one specific technique that you want to focus on and cover in an hour. Depending on prior knowledge and level of performance, you can train your group on this technique within various complex contexts (vis-à-vis position, distances, direction of movements, links with other techniques, cooperative or less cooperative partners, etc.).

Table 1: The methods matrix

Type of attack / Distance and positioning work	Direct	Combination/ Series	Broken rhythm	Indirect (with feint)	Immobilization
Linear					
Square formation					
Moving in a circle • Clockwise • Counterclockwise					
Principle of attack angle • Simple					
• Composite (Zig-zag principle)					

Here is an example:

The main technique for the session of one hour is mae-geri.

Your students practice the technique from the different linear directions of movement (forward, backward, sideways). This gives them a basic understanding of combining the technique with preparatory movements.

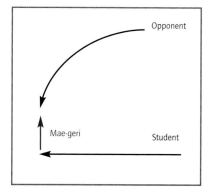

Our example: The opponent circles around the student. The student "cuts" into this circular movement with a step sideways and does a mae-geri kick.

Diagram 22

The student has to move freely when in the circle with his partner. He delivers the mae-geri kick at the right moment from the correct distance. Finding this correct distance is what the student must achieve.

When training for the principle of attack angles, the student has to internalize the fact that he always goes away from the direct attack line. The zig-zag principle means that he will never attack his opponent in a straight line but will leave the direct attack line once or several times. Alternatively, he may break through the line and thus disturb the opponent's orientation (see Chapter 1.4.5 "Pushing through the attack"; it's the same principle!).

Your students can use the mae-geri as a *single technique (direct attack)* or combine it with other techniques. Students link 2-4 techniques. In the first step, they combine the techniques fluently with each other *(combination/series)*. In the next step, they build in delays, acceleration, and mini pauses *(broken rhythm)*.
A didactic analogy: Let your students recite a normal sentence to their training partner at a normal rate. In the next step, they have to stutter and include various pauses as they say the sentence. The listeners can no longer predict which syllables or words will follow next. They are confused.

In the *indirect (with feints)* version, your student executes 1-2 techniques in the combination/series *incompletely*. In this case, the opponent is led to expect the feinted technique (he automatically thinks that it has been executed as a complete one). The student can thus employ the crucial mae-geri technique earlier than expected by the opponent.

In *immobilization,* your student prevents the opponent from changing his distance and undertaking any defensive actions, such as elbow control. Immobilization always means reducing the scope of action by the opponent by holding, causing loss of balance, and taking advantage of the environment (using a wall, corner, ground obstacles, etc.). In our example, the student can deliver a short-distance mae-geri kick under the elbows.

2.2.5.7   Using Training Aids

The Coaching Mitt

The coaching mitt is a tool that allows the fighter to develop more precision, as well as act as an aid to increase his perception and decision-making power. Although he can attack the coaching mitt with great force, the fighter's primary goal should not be to increase his strike strength with their aid. In the coaching mitt, the fighter has a good and handy tool with which he can train anywhere. He can use them to simulate combat situations and he can also gain the feeling for the right moment of attack (timing), distance, position and exploitation of gaps.

Some tips for working with the coaching mitt:
*   *Always* warm-up before starting your training and *stretch* for a short period (depending on the intended exercise to be done).
*   As the person wearing the coaching mitt, always take into consideration the flexibility and experience of the person exercising.
*   Slowly raise the demands on the flexibility of the person practicing. Start with a medium rate and increase it until the person practicing reaches his limit.
*   *Precision* has priority over *force*. The beginner should only increase his striking force once his precision is right and he can correctly judge his distance and position.
*   As the person wearing the coaching mitt, point to clearly defined targets. If your partner is a little unclear, or he is afraid to hit you with his technique, he will not properly execute the technique.

Two basic ways to hold the coaching mitt:
*   Especially with beginners, highlight the targets *in front* of your body. This way you can prevent being hit or injured.
*   With advanced students, highlight the target directly *on your body.* This way, you enable the student practicing to estimate a realistic distance to the target.

In order to increase the degree of complexity and difficulty, we recommend teaching the following sequence:
*   The person wearing the coaching mitt (trainer) and the person exercising (student) adopt firm positions. The student must now concentrate on executing the technique or combination correctly.
*   The trainer remains static while the student can move around. The student now has to additionally integrate legwork into his technique. Key question: What step do you use to bridge the given distance the best?
*   Both move. The student now has to attack a moving, evading target. Practicing this type of exercise develops movement patterns, which he can also use in a fight.
*   The trainer moves freely about and actively engages in an attack with either a previously determined or alternatively undisclosed technique. While he does this or shortly after, he indicates a target for the partner's counterattack.

Here are the most common drills using the coaching mitt:

Training Shot

The person exercising (student) executes one or two agreed-upon techniques at maximum speed at the coaching mitt. When the person wearing the coaching mitt (trainer) keeps it hidden, this is the moment to look at the reaction rate. The student needs to react "explosively" in the shortest possible time once the target has been indicated. You can carry out this training in the form of a simple decision-making exercise (for example, it is unclear whether a right or a left mawashi-geri is required), alternatively the trainer should vary the height at which he holds the mitt.

The more advanced the student is, the freer the trainer can indicate targets thus making it more fight-realistic.

Speed Drills

In a short, defined period (10, 15, 20, 30 seconds), the student has to carry out as many techniques as rapidly as possible.

Alternate version:

The student carries out a defined number of techniques in the shortest possible time.

"Telegraphing"

The idea behind this exercise is simple: The student delivers his kicking or punching techniques faster than the trainer anticipates or can react to. This form of exercise trains the fighter to deliver techniques without any preparatory movements.

The trainer tries to pull the coaching mitt back (but only at a moderate speed to avoid injury).

Combination Drills

The student joins 2-5 combinations and techniques in a series together. The trainer ensures that one technique moves into the next without interrupting the flow. Here, too, 1-2 techniques can be predetermined and the remainder will be chosen based on the situation.

Rapid-Fire Drills

The student has to carry out 10-20 techniques, such as kinteki-geri, mawashi-geri as fast as possible, one after the other. This drill promotes stamina and the ability to carry out a continuous attack. The target is either given in advance or is determined during the practice (right/left, up/down).

Counter Drills

The trainer attacks using a predetermined technique (or freely) and indicates targets on his own body with the mitt for one or two counter techniques.

These drills are used to practice speed, timing, coordination, balance, precision, reflex training and judging situations.

Arm Protectors, Air-Shields, Punching Bag

The objective of the training in using these tools is to improve *power specifically* (specifically here means full contact specific force). We recommend 3-5 *sets or each with 6-8 repetitions.* If your focus is on endurance specifically, then use a series of 10, 15, 20 or 30 seconds duration. The training drills that we covered for the coaching mitt can also be used here with a changed focus.

Examples for training with the arm protectors:

In the following examples, you can easily see that you can practice good combinations of hand and foot techniques with the arm protectors. Training sessions using only the smaller coaching mitts are appropriate where only hand techniques are being trained. The wearer can act and respond more quickly with them and thus simulate attacks and gaps for attacks. He can get closer to the real fight than when using the arm protectors.

By training with the arm protectors, the force component in the technique is stressed. Training with the coaching mitt focuses on speed and tactics.

An example of decision-making training follows:
Decision-making training means that we must consider which technique should be carried out, as it is not certain from the outset. By virtue of the neutral start position, the person exercising (student) must immediately register in his mind which technique is called for and then execute it as quickly as possible.

Neutral start position

The technique is delivered dependent on the way the protector is being held.

The person holding the protector (trainer) can also actively intervene and simulate a combat situation. In the following example, he delivers a swinging strike at the student's head with the pad. The student has to do a U-turn to evade the attack and then counter directly.

The following three photos show an example of the combination of knee and fist

It is good that the entire body weight is behind the final technique.

Using the oversized punching bag (seen in the following photos), you can practice techniques with full effort. The focus is clearly on developing the punch.

The long punching bag allows the fighters to practice the full repertoire of Full Contact Karate techniques from low kicks to punches. The emphasis clearly lies in the development of penetrating force.

Jump Rope

The use of the jump rope improves:
*   Stamina
*   Hand-foot coordination
*   Breathing rhythm
*   The feeling for the rhythm of movement
*   Legwork

The right way to jump rope: Your upper arms lightly touch the sides of your body. You swing the rope only by rotating the wrists.
　　　　The jumps (skipping actions) are done only by the ankle joints and only the balls of your feet are in contact with the ground.

Various ways to jump rope:
*   With both legs
*   On one leg
*   Crossing over the arms as you skip
*   Crossing your legs as you skip
*   Swing the rope twice for each jump
*   Alter the position of your legs as you skip (changeover legs once to the right then left and then to the rear and vice versa)
*   Bring the knees up to your chest as you skip
*   Bring your heels up to your bottom as you skip

Jumping rope is good for a general warm-up when you note the following points:
- Jump at least 5 cm off the ground.
- Jump only on the balls of your feet. **Don't** let your heels touch the floor.
- Keep your shoulders relaxed and maintain an upright position. The quicker your rhythm, the more compact your posture.
- At the beginning, skip 3-6 times a minute. Gradually increase to 1-3 times for 3 minutes with a one-minute pause between each set.
- As you skip, change speed and rhythm. Do little spurts at top speed. Do this for less than 8-10 seconds so that you stay in the anaerobic (non-lactic) zone or, in other words, so that you don't over-tax your body.
- In an ideal case, check your pulse using a blood pressure machine.

Medicine Ball

A Karateka, who is preparing for a full contact fight must gradually attune himself to cope with punches and kicks without being injured. When he is hit, he must not lose his fighting spirit nor his will to win. In Full Contact Karate, the fighters aim at the body and the legs. Advanced Karateka are able to fight with 60-80% of their full strength. The student has to develop certain patterns so that he can absorb the opponent's techniques. This includes breathing out explosively at the moment of being hit in combination with the tensing of the intercostal and abdominal muscles. Using the medicine ball helps to exercise the body and get it used to the full contact techniques. Equally, the medicine ball can serve as an aid to activate the muscle chain in the body needed for punches.

Examples of toughening up exercises:
- Both partners stand 1.5-2m opposite of each other. One of the partners throws the medicine ball directly at the other's stomach. (Note: The passive partner protects his head and genitals.)
- One partner stands by the side of the other lying down and lets the medicine ball fall or throws it onto the other's stomach or ribcage. The passive partner breathes out forcibly and tenses his muscles just prior to contact with the ball. (Repeat 20-25 times then switch partner roles.)
- One partner is lying down and the other is standing over him and strikes the other's middle with the medicine ball.

Throwing exercises:
- Exercise with a partner: There is 5-10m between them depending on the strength of the throw. The ball is thrust in front of the partner's chest using both arms. Feet are kept parallel. (Repeat 6-8 times and as soon as the explosiveness of the exercise wanes, take a break.)
- Left foot forward or right foot forward:
  One-arm throw on the side of the forward foot (oi-tsuki).

Throw on the side of the rear leg (gyaku-tsuki).
(Repeat 6-8 times.)
* The partners stand back to back.
* Move the ball in a curve and pass it back over the head or through the legs.

Mirror

The mirror is a training aid for the advanced student. It practices the control of:

* Fighting posture and cover
* Movement
* Technique

Because the student can watch his technique execution in the mirror, he gets direct feedback about the categories we have mentioned. Naturally, this will only work if the student can see with his mind the precise movement pattern that he should be doing and compare it with what he sees.

The aims of training with a mirror are as follows:

* Improving his *cover* when standing and being aware of gaps in it when he is moving.
* The effectiveness of feints. Are they realistic enough to entice the opponent into the required reaction?
* Precision in the interplay between legwork, dodging maneuvers and evading movements. Are they being done economically enough and are there any superfluous movements?

Using the mirror, the instructor can give the beginner direct feedback about his mistakes.

The advanced student can correct his own mistakes using the mirror because he already has a vision of the correct (hopefully!) technique pattern in his mind's eye and therefore has an idea of what he has to do.

2.2.5.8 Developing Punching Strength

In Full Contact Karate, it is not enough to be able to show off nice, artistic techniques that strike you as strange in order to win. To KO your opponent in a fight or to knock him down onto the ground with the effectiveness of your strike, you must execute the technique in a coordinated manner along the lines of certain principles.

Newton's second law says:

$F = m \times a$
(where F = Power, m = mass, a = acceleration).

Don't worry – we'll keep it plain and simple!

Because acceleration (a) can also be described as a change of speed in a particular time *(t)*, thus, $(\Delta v / \Delta t)$, the formula above can also be written as:

$$F = m \times \frac{v}{t}$$

We can convert this into:

$$\mathbf{F \times t = m \times v}$$

The careful reader will now ask whenever possible (as he sits bored to tears) what the devil has this to do with fighting. The formula describes the impulse that you pass on to an opponent when using a technique. The only quantity that is not influenced in this equation is the mass of the driving force; everything else is variable. The higher the speed with which you punch or kick, the higher value on the right side of the equation and similarly the left side. If we assume that the product of "F x t" is constant (for a given mass and speed), then the power released is increased by it so that the *effective time is kept for the shortest time at the target* (F↑ x t↓ = F x t).

The conclusions that we reach for the development of force in a technique are:

- *Fast speed* in the execution (only possible with relaxation of the non-participating muscles → optimum technique) and
- *Short effect.*

This is in an ideal situation. You will not be able to achieve this in every fight situation or with every technique. Different tactical demands often work on a limited basis. However, you now know the theoretical background about what influences the penetrating force of a technique. You can also now analyze weak points that have to be improved.

When we used the formula above, we assumed a constant mass for the driving force (for example, the arm or the leg). In fighting that is only partially correct because the fighter can increase the mass in an individual technique by bringing his whole body into play.

An oi technique gets its force by *"translation (straight line movement) of the center of balance of the body"* in the direction of the target and not by stretching the arm alone. A gyaku technique uses *"rotation"* combined with the stretching out of the rear leg made possible by pushing off from the ball of the foot.

In practice, the fighter combines translation and rotation.

In an ideal case, the attack angle should be 90° to the area of the target. Any deviation from this angle lessens the effect but may be necessary because of tactical demands or requirements of the situation.

In traditional Karate, there is the concept of *kime*, i.e., all the muscles are tensed at the moment of the strike and for a split second the body forms a monolithic block. The theory for this can be found in the physics of Newton's third law *action = reaction*. Put simply, this means the more force that you use to hit an object (body, board, wall, etc.), the more resulting counterforce is created, which is effective in the part of the body that is attacking. If there are weak spots in your own attacking "system" (in the muscle chain and joints for a particular technique) then the whole force will not develop as it reaches the target. It is then quite possible that the attacker will injure himself (twisted wrist, lack of tension in the buttocks and wrong alignment when kicking, all leading to a loss of balance). Explosiveness in the muscle chain in the legs, tensing of the buttock muscles and the striking force of the limbs of the body must all be molded into a single functioning unit.

If the fighter wants to attain his *optimum speed*, he has to keep all those muscles that are not involved in a *relaxed state* right up until he hits the target. If he tenses his muscles too early, there will be a resultant slowing in his movements and thus a weakening of his strike.

Depth of penetration into the target is also a decisive factor. The aim is to strike *into the target to a depth of 10-20cms* and not just onto the target. Karate styles that do not use the coaching mitt, etc., to train do not develop any effective strength. The data in literature regarding the optimum depth of penetration for a technique varies widely. For many students, it is therefore a question of finding his own individual optimum strike and not be put off doing so.

We recommend you have another look at the diagrams in Chapter 1.4.3 "Resolving Problems in a Fight Situation" where we illustrated the elements of optimum use of the transfer of strength (see Page 24).

2.2.5.9 Additional Technical Training to Improve Coordination

By using the term *"additional technical training,"* we mean the measures that a student employs only indirectly to improve his fighting ability, but which optimize the variety of techniques the student can use. In the end, the fighter can adapt his techniques better in different fight situations thanks to this training element. Besides this, these methodical measures afford variety in training.

- Change of *movement direction*
Stepping forward, backwards, sideways, diagonally and circling as a lead-up to the technique.

- Changing *the strike angle*
For example, in mawashi-geri, 90° to the target, 45° downward.

- Changing *speed* and *rhythm*
Different speeds, broken rhythm, maximum speed at the beginning, abrupt break in movements.

- Change in *effort*
Training using various types of coaching mitts/punching bags, accentuation of force in a series (first or second or third techniques are especially hard).

- Change of *movement amplitude*
Executing a technique at long distance, short distance.

Key question: How do I adapt the technique so that I can still hit the target with force?
To do this, the student has to work out for himself the individual distance (which shortest distance, longest distance can be the most effective for the technique).

- Changes in *other conditions*
Executing techniques on grass, sand, asphalt, wooden floors, in water, uphill, downhill, on stairs, with the hands fixed into the belt, etc.

- Changes in the *details of a movement*
Particular details of the movement are over-accentuated, the movement is broken up into individual phases, practiced with pauses between the phases, e.g., turning the hips in a lot – stop – kick – stop, pull back the kicking foot – stop – hips back.

- Practicing only the *weaker side* in training

- Using predetermined start situations

- **Training with *continually changing situations***

Against several opponents, attacking in-line, against a heralded attack, selected attacks (2-3 attack techniques in the selection), free fight attacks.

- **Executing techniques *after a work-out***

For example, do 10 push-ups or 20 knee-bends or a similar exercise, and then do the technique.

- **Executing a technique after *losing (or slightly losing) your balance***

Eyes shut, arms pinned down, turning around quickly 10 times, being pulled back by the partner while doing a technique, after doing several forward rolls or backward rolls – then do the technique.

- ***Limitation of space***

Fight in a 4-square meter area, nobody is allowed to step into a "forbidden" circular area during the fight, in a boxing ring.

- ***Making the technique difficult to perform by having to do an unusual movement beforehand***

Jodan-mawashi-geri after a handstand, cartwheel, or doing a spin.

- ***Unusual starting positions***

From lying on the stomach, on the back, kneeling, standing on one leg, back to the partner, standing one leg on a chair/bank or similar position.

2.2.5.10   Developing Speed

Speed is a key factor for the ability of a full contact fighter. The prerequisite for speed includes an ***informatory*** and an *energetic* element.

The element relative to "informatory" is *the speed of reaction.* By this, we mean the interval of time between the initial perception of a stimulus and the beginning of the reaction to it. Speed of reaction is *genetically determined* and therefore can only be trained for with limitation (general stimulus). With reference to speed of reaction to general stimuli, there is hardly any difference between a highly trained fighter and a man in the street.

It is quite different, however, when other specific stimuli are present (e.g., jodan- mawashi-geri). Here, the reaction time is much shorter than that of the man in the street. This has to do with the fighting experience of the Karateka, where the reaction time is influenced or superimposed by anticipation and intuition, or gained from knowledge and a thousand repetitions of the situation. A clear difference of which factor comes into play, and by how much, for the reaction time cannot be made.

Reaction time can be roughly sub-divided into three phases:

1.   **Unspecific perception**
Note that something has happened.

2.   **Processing phase**
Identifying type of attack, speed, difficulty, attack angle, etc.

3.   **Selection of counteraction phase**
Deciding which appropriate defense, evading maneuver, counterattack to use. This phase depends very much upon previous knowledge, experience, technical ability, quickness in making decisions and realistic assessment of one's own abilities.

Full Contact Karate actions are irregular movement actions (in contrast to cycling, swimming and the like). The speed of movement or the time required for a maneuver depends on the following factors:

*   *Relaxation*, i.e., only those muscles work that are involved in the movement. Relaxation follows in the necessary period of time, and involves optimum coordination of the movement.
*   *Correct technique*, i.e., economical movement path.
*   *Rapid hip movement/Rotation* with transference to moving the limbs.
*   *Will/Quickness in making decisions* → "All or nothing" principle.

According to research by Soviet boxing trainers (see Degtjarow & Dsherojan, 1979) there are four independent categories of speed:

1.   Speed of reaction
2.   Speed of an individual technique
3.   Speed of the combination/series
4.   Speed of legwork/positioning

As an instructor, this means that you analyze the student and establish where he has gaps and in which category. You then work specifically on building these up.

Similarly, you should particularly work on training legwork and anticipation often. This category is extremely important because reaction time takes longer than the time required for execution.

2.2.5.11   Strength Training for Full Contact Fighters

As a full contact fighter, your muscles have a different meaning to those of a body builder. A body builder strives to build up voluminous amounts of muscle, while your muscles function as armor plating. What does this mean?

If I am successful in building up several kilos of muscle by training, then these muscles are protection for the joints and, contrary to previous opinion, this gives me a higher level of power to be able to develop improved explosive force. Certain techniques, such as jodan-mawashi-geri, cannot be executed forcefully enough without well-developed gluteal muscles (smaller and middle gluteal muscles) and the ability to keep the buttocks stable. In the following passages, we show you exercises that train the important muscle groups without having to use much apparatus. The selection of items is not necessarily complete. If you want to find out more about this complex subject then we recommend you research it further in the large amount of literature available.

For systematic reasons, we begin with the leg muscles as they are a large group of muscles that have an effect on the other muscle groups when training on your own. We then move onto the remaining muscle groups in order of importance up finally to the upper body group.

Legs

By maintaining a stretched arm posture (upper arms are at the height of the ears), tension is created in the back and this is increased by bending the knees. It is important that the coccyx is pushed well to the rear while the lower legs remain virtually vertical. **Concept:** I am going to sit right back on to a stool.

Mistakes:

- The arms wander forward because it is more comfortable → reduction of tension in the back.
- The lower legs are not kept vertical → not ideal for the knee.

You can increase the intensity further by executing this move while bending only one knee. Be sure to keep your back straight, breastbone out forward ("Show me your medals!") and lower legs remain vertical.

In the following exercise, you combine bending one knee only (standing up) with a stretching and rotation of the spinal cord in the chest area.

Push the one leg lunged out to the rear. This way it is easier to keep the forward lower leg vertical and also avoid overtaxing the knee.

Reach up, twisting the lower back and chest spinal area up and around. (Good for desk-bound workers!!)

Come back up into the parallel standing position by using the force from the leg by pushing up on the forward one.

A further exercise comprises plyometric training for leg muscles:

Plyometric training means the rapid transfer from the stretch cycle over to the shortening cycle of the muscles. Do three short jumps. At the third jump, drop down onto your knees and stop the downward movement approximately at the height as the two Karateka in the picture. You follow this by either stretching directly back up (Concept: "Ouch! I've sat down on a sharp pin!"), or you pause for a second or two in a half-squat and then push back up explosively.

Rear Muscle Group

In the following exercises, we train the rear thigh muscles, the buttock muscles and the lower back.

When the knee joints are bent at 90° or less, the main tension is felt in the buttock muscles and in the lower back. By increasing the angle of the knee joints over 90°, you place a demand mainly on the rear upper thigh muscles (the ischiocrural muscles, or the hamstrings). Lifting the pelvis higher using one leg makes the exercise very intensive.

Hold your body arched over the floor.

Front Muscle Group

This exercise gives us the possibility to train for the strengthening of the stomach muscles and diagonal coordination.

Starting position: Push the feet against an imaginary wall and push the hands forward. **Note:** Your shoulders remain permanently in the air and never touch the floor.

Execution: Push one heel flat over the floor and stretch the diagonal arm out to the rear. You stabilize the position of the pelvis using the drawn-up bent leg. In the stretching phase, hold this position for 2-3 seconds and then slowly change over.

In order to train the diagonal stomach muscles (flanking muscles), when you change over, twist a little to the side.

The next exercise:

Relatively easy version of an exercise for the forward muscle group

The harder version

The further the distance between the hands and the feet, the harder it is to maintain a stable position. As soon as you notice that your back begins to sag, end the exercise.

The mountain climber:

In the push-up position, pull the knee up to the chest alternately.

Balancing on your buttocks, slowly roll backward on your backbone, vertebra by vertebra. With a little force, come back up into the balancing position. To make it easier, you can help yourself by hooking your forefinger into the hollow behind your knee. To do the harder version, complete the exercise with your arms open. You must keep the tension in your stomach muscles for as long as needed for you to be able to swing back up into the balancing position without the help of your arms.

Side Muscle Group

In the following section, we show you a basic exercise along with variations according to difficulty. In exercises 1-3, please note that you only use the edge of the foot to press onto the floor and that the ankle joint is lifted off the ground.

Side support with leg lifted

In this variation, the goal is to train the diagonal stomach muscles, the smaller and middle buttock muscles and the outside muscles of the legs. From the starting position, do little hip pushes toward the ceiling. This places the side of the body facing the floor under dynamic strain. A static loading of the muscle occurs in the leg lifted on the other side. Doing this places high demands on your strength and coordination. If it is too difficult for you then do the following:

Place the feet over each other and concentrate on doing the hip movements upward.

If you cannot keep your balance, then do the exercise like this:

Place the legs, one behind the other, thus increasing the supported area. Move the hips again.

A further simplified way to complete exercise 1 is to angle the leg on the floor.

When you do this exercise with a partner, you can help each other or even make it harder.

Supportive

The pitiless variation

Small of the Back

The next exercise is called "rowing on dry land"

You place the elbows on the ground near your ribs and curve your breastbone and belly button toward the ceiling.

Concept: Imagine that a little mouse must be able to run between your back and the floor without injuring itself. Press your head into your neck so that you can stretch your body fully. Straight away you are working with your back and not with your stomach muscles.

Starting position   Pressing up from the floor

Dropping back down again   Variation with the elbows placed out wider

The Complete Rear Muscle Group

In the next exercise, the ball is moved in a Figure 8 over the backs of the two people exercising. If you stretch your feet up, the exercise becomes more difficult. (Just lift up only a little. It's about getting tall!)

Chest, Shoulders and Triceps

When doing a push-up, irrespective of type, it is always important that:
- You maintain body tension.
- You don't sag in the middle.

If you want to train for *stamina* then do a high number of repetitions (30-50).
If you want to train *for explosive speed and maximum strength* then do a maximum of 4-6 repeats.

One way of doing *explosive speed and strength* training is to slowly adopt a low push-up position. Pause in this posture and then explosively push yourself up.

For *maximum strength* training, all variations are suitable that only use one arm.

In the following section, we show some variations and combinations of push-up exercises.

Four-point contact with the floor – fists and feet

Three-point contact with the floor – one leg is lifted up. This makes the exercise more difficult.

A similar three-point contact version

Variation done on the tips of the fingers

Push-up with arched back in U form

  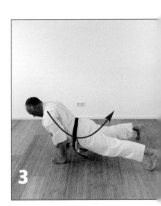

This version of the push-up is good training for your shoulders. Furthermore, it places demands on stabilizing your whole body.

The next version is designed to train your balance using a fitness ball or a small ball:

Balance one arm on the ball on one side so that you place some pressure on the other arm propped up to the side.

The last push-up exercise is a combination exercise:

Bring your knee up sideways into the armpit. The arms must now support the weight of the body.

Twist up sideways from the arm support.

The sideways support requires you to concentrate on keeping your balance because the supporting area is very small.

Upper Back

A weak upper back often leaves its mark (especially among desk-bound workers). Therefore, this is exactly why training these muscles is important.

Start by leaning against the wall. Feet are away from the wall. The further they are away from the wall, the harder the exercise.

Hold your body as stiff as a board and push away from the wall (only about 5-10cms) with your elbows. The shoulder blades move in toward your backbone and the breastbone is still pushed forward.

Another exercise:

Starting position: Hold the fists pointing inward (thumbs pointing toward the feet).

Push the elbows up toward the ceiling. Your fists leave the floor.

Different ways to hold the arms

Another version with arms outstretched

Neck

Press against your partner's head using a shotei. He presses back against it.

Jump around

Do the same with the other hand

Careful! Don't ram your fingers into your opponent's eyes! Also, don't hit him, but just keep the pressure on your partner's head. In any case, he is bound to get his revenge on you!

Isometric exercises for the neck

Forward   Backwards

To the side

Slowly build up pressure against your hands – hold for 8-10 seconds and then let loose. Hold your head firmly. Watch out if you have neck problems.

Calves

With this last exercise for a relatively small muscle, we conclude the series.

One foot is lifted up. Make sure you have plenty of room to control your movements. Hold the foot up at its highest point for about a second. **Important:** At the highest point, stand on the ball of the big toe. To do this, you have to turn your foot inward a little (pronation).

2.2.5.12 Sparring Training with Tactical Exercises

In this form of fight training, you break down the complex situation of a real fight into simple situations and tasks. The emphasis lies in the tactical solutions and not on exerting force or pure power of self-assertion. The advantage for the fighter is that he will learn to be able to solve complex fighting actions with ever-increasing knowledge. This way he checks himself and comes to terms, step by step, with the correct way to fight. He reduces the risk of fear and injury that would cause him to abandon his path toward becoming a good fighter. The aim is to learn to "fight with brains" and not to give the opponent a "roasting" by sheer force.

When you give your student tactical problems, you will get results from the following:

- His strategic/tactical knowledge will be systematically expanded
- His joy at fighting will grow
- His fear will subside

Against this background, sparring is an interesting, demanding and hard sport that one can even compare to chess. The student can use his knowledge, apply his strongest techniques and practice his weak points in detail. You can guard against overtaxing your student by giving him adequate tactical problems to solve. The key to success is that the student has fun sparring. However, a demanding and responsible-minded sparring partner is required for this.

Attack and Counterattack Variations in Relation to the Opponent's Actions

Direct Attack

As soon as the student exercising has reached the correct distance and position, he attacks.

Direct Attack Using Preparatory Leg Work

The training partner acts cooperatively.

When he presents a *static target*, the student has to judge the exact distance and adjust it using the correct legwork. The aim is to get a feeling for which steps are best used to bridge which distance.

If the partner presents a *moving target* then care must be taken with beginners that they are capable of predicting the changes necessary in position and distance. The training partner can increase the demands and get nearer to real fighting actions once the student has made more progress.

Direct Attack Using Preparatory Leg Work and Combining Feints

The student executes a feint. The training partner reacts to it. Depending on his reaction, the student now has to decide the form of his subsequent direct attack.

Key Questions:

- What gap has the feint made in the partner's cover?
- What fine-tuning or modification of the technique is needed to be able to attack this target?

The partner can respond as previously agreed or freely.

Practicing the Complete Fight Sequence
(Leg Work, Execution, Pushing Through the Attack)

In this form of training, the partner tries to counterattack. The student has to try unpredictably to get out of the direct attack line or use a different measure to push the attack through.

Continuous Attack

This is a form of a "mugging" attack. The student fires off 4-6 rapid attacks in quick succession. This overfeeds the partner with information and allows the attacker to land 1-2 successful techniques.

Attack – Reaction – Attack

The partner's reaction to the first attack by the student determines the form of the latter's second attack.

Feint – Attack

In all probability, a feint will cause a particular reaction so that the student can anticipate the gap it creates and gain a tactical advantage meaning the partner is *rendered helpless for a second*. The question here is not who is quicker, but rather who can *plausibly* place his partner in a position to have to make a disadvantageous move through false information.

Counterattack Following an Attack

This is a classic form of exercise with a drawn-out time structure. However, it is too slow without simultaneous helping actions (such as increasing the length of the attack movement, immobilization, putting off balance) for the real fight. It presents a good introduction to the subject in the opening teaching sessions.

Simultaneous Counterattack

This has to do with an artificially trained movement. The training partner attacks the student who moves into this attack, dodging minimally to one side and at the same time going into a counterattack. It is particularly difficult here to withstand the impulse to back away from the attack. This form of training places high demands on one's feeling for time ('timing'), the ability to anticipate and the student's determination.

Preemptive Attack Against an Anticipated Attack

This is the most demanding form of the counterattack. The prerequisite for it is that the student can "read" the partner's preparatory attack pattern and catch his developing attack "cold." Here it is also crucial that sufficient speed, concentration, cold-bloodedness and determination are present in order to put this tactic into action.

Practicing Tactical Patterns

A tactical pattern is an artificially isolated part of a complex fighting situation. These patterns crop up in a more or less pure form in any fight. The goal of training for these is to keep control over the situation while considering time pressure, pressure of decisiveness and the rapid delivery of precise actions for the techniques. The students learn to recognize such patterns during a fight and use them to their advantage.

1 : 1 (Single Technique in Response to a Single Technique)

The student responds to each of the partner's techniques with one of his own. Carry this out at top speed and precision for 10, 15, 20, 30 or 60 seconds. If the emphasis is more on the aspect of speed then shorter periods are preferable.

2 : 1 (Double Attack Against a Single Counterattack)

The counterattack can be delivered between the two attacks or afterwards. Correct timing is crucially important here.

1 : 2 (Double Counterattack Against a Single Attack)

The student aims at gaps in the attacker's cover with targeted counterattacks.

1 : 1 : 1 (Attack – Counterattack – Counterattack)

In this maneuver, one mentally trains the rapid changeover of roles between attacker and defender. If you simply don't react, but rather anticipate the probable counterattack employed by the partner then this will be a technique of secondary intention.

2 : 1 : 1 (Double Attack – Counterattack – Counterattack)

Intention is as the previous structures described, but the number of techniques is increased.

1 : 1 : 1 : 1 (Attack - Counterattack - Counterattack - Counterattack)

Key question: Who scores the point?

The last three forms of techniques described specifically train you in the ability to adapt quickly to whatever situation you are in.

Training with Fixed Timed Bouts

For this method of sparring, the student has to score a point inside the shortest possible time (15 seconds, 30 seconds or the like). This forces him to target and exploit the gaps left by the opponent. He is also under time pressure. Using half or full force, the opponent can act *cooperatively, provocatively* or *with resistance*. This is dependent upon the student's technical prowess and level of performance. The partner is also jointly responsible for his opponent's progress.

Other variations for this type of tactical task include:

*   Score two strikes in 20 seconds.
*   Score a point using a left jodan-mawashi-geri inside a minute.

Handicap Training

A handicap is given to a fighter, when, in relation to his opponent he is superior to him or when he is forced by an artificial limitation to use his weaker techniques (or work from his weaker side).

Examples:

*   The left hand is pinned to the back of his belt.
*   The fighter may kick only with his right foot.
*   The fighter may only dodge *without* using defensive actions.

Pre-planned Training

Prior to the sparring bout, the student is asked what technique he wants to use to score. Stress is created by the fact that the student has to plan to score with this technique in the shortest possible time, while he realizes that the opponent already knows which one he will use.

"One-shot" Training

The student has only one chance to score. This type of training helps to develop willpower, rapid decision making, concentration, keeping a cool head and furthers the idea of "all or nothing."

Free Sparring Using Hidden Strategies

The instructor prescribes what strategy the student should use for the sparring bout (e.g., be only defensive, disrupt all of the opponent's starts, only use a mawashi-geri or similar). The other student has to recognize the strategy being used during the sparring and then tell the instructor which one it was.

Two-man Kumite

The aim of two-man kumite is to train staying power, stamina, willpower and specifically the problems of distance and position. The student always has to try to position himself so that he keeps one opponent between himself and the other opponent. This develops the ability to keep a good overview of complex situations, as well as learning to disregard the opponent's strikes and maintain absolute willpower. An exercise form only for the advanced!

Sabaki (turning the body)

This is where a student stands in the middle of a circle surrounded by 4-6 partners. The students around the circle attack the one in the center of the circle with force one after the other. The student in the middle has to recognize the attacks straight away and, without hesitation, counterattack. This calls for a "direct answer" to the "question" (fight situation). There is no time to consciously apply solutions; instead, the "answers" come from the repertoire of trained, ingrained patterns of movement. What happens here is a "reduction of the complexity" (of the situation) into a number of "nodes," followed up by a direct reply. The sabaki is an extremely demanding physical form of exercise.

2.2.6 The Techniques and Their Movements

A technique in a combat situation is not an isolated element or module. It is connected to a network of preparatory, deceptive and protective activities in different situational contexts. For most of the techniques we present, we include a diagram. The technique is shown centrally as the key element. Grouped around it are the preparatory moves, protective and deception actions and possible combinations of techniques.

This gives you a handy aid with which you can structure the technique better. You can pick out certain aspects, accentuate them and practice the technique "pre-packaged" so to speak. This way you avoid boredom, and all students learn much more about a technique than they would have conducting a simple improvement in their basic training.

The units of action involved makes up the totality of possible actions around which a central technique is formed. They can be broken down into chains of action and practiced in the best way to fit you (individually) or your students. Together you can be creative and develop your own chains of action. The units of action are not necessarily complete and may be seen from the viewpoint of Bruce Lee:

"Absorb what is useful, reject what is useless, add your own!"

2.2.6.1   Feints

A feint is defined as a misleading piece of information about a subsequent action. If you execute a feint, you have misled (at best) your opponent to make a reaction that favors your own intentions.
    The feint has several advantages: You make a sudden action from a position or distance that catches your opponent unaware. Or you disturb your opponent's perception and situation analysis, thus putting his rhythm off.

Why does a feint work? Human perception has the tendency to complete incomplete information on a confirmation bias basis. This is supplemented by knowledge and experience. This also means that beginners cannot easily respond to subtle deceptions because they lack the necessary experience and background.

You gain the advantage of time and space by using a feint. Your opponent delays his response or drops his guard. Either that or you bridge distances surprisingly quickly. Jakhel (1989) calls this situation a tactical moment (TM), a state of reduced responsiveness. If your opponent is more experienced, then you can use subtler feints because you provoke certain reactions using them. Feints are therefore ideal for finding out what makes up your opponent's reaction pattern.

By using feints, you can cover the following parameters:
1.   Spatial
2.   Time
3.   Use of force
4.   The opponent's psychological state
5.   Technical

Here are a few examples:

1. **Spatial parameters**
   - Change from lengthening distance to shortening distance. Switch between a low angle of attack (low kick) to head attacks, from right to left, using different angles of attack, and more.

2. **Time parameters**
   - Use slowly executed feints against very fast attacks. The intention here is to accustom the opponent to relatively slow movements in order to surprise him with your speed of attack.
   - Move from predictable rhythm to broken rhythm.

3. **Use of force parameters**
   Use multiple relaxed feints at half speed, then use hard attacks with full force.

4. **The opponent's psychological state**
   - By uttering a kiai (battle cry), this gives the opponent a brief shock for a fraction of a second after which he relaxes. Move into the attack in this relaxation phase.
   - Put on a show, i.e., fake fatigue or fear. When the opponent attacks then consequently counterattack.
   - Dropping your cover leads to the opening of certain gaps into which the opponent can attack. Move into this attack.
   - Aim at gaps opened by the opponent, but attack a different target area.

Practicing feints is just as important as practicing the technique itself! Preparing for the coup de grace and the final technique cannot be overestimated. Therefore, you must integrate practicing feints into the technical and tactical combat training. It is not the brilliant technician who wins the fight, but the fighter who can best conceal his intended techniques through feints!

5. **Technical parameters**
   A technical feint is defined as the combination of several techniques where the first technique is performed incompletely. You interrupt the movements of the first technique abruptly thus steering the opponent's attention or anticipation onto a wrong target region. For example, you can change the trajectory of the technique half way through (from a mae-geri to mawashi-geri). For this reason, we recommend that you do your kicks from the same lead-up so that the opponent remains uncertain about the technique you are using until the last moment (Bill Wallace is an example of someone who does this well).

Here is a short summary for practicing feints:

- **Body feints**
  You make a feint by moving the shoulders or pelvis.

- **Technique feints**

  You stop a technique suddenly in the middle of the movement and go into a different technique.

- **Feint using distance**

  You lengthen and/or shorten the distance to the opponent in an unpredictable manner.

- **Angular feints**

  You check that you have come out of the direct line of combat and then you attack from a different, slightly varying angle. As an extension of the angular feint, you can change the angle 2-3 times (zig-zag principle), thus causing the opponent to keep having to reorient himself.

- **Visual feint**

  You look at a particular place and strike at another. (Ineffective on experienced fighters!)

- **Audible feints**

  You utter a battle cry (kiai), then wait a split second. What happens? The opponent expects an attack. If you don't execute one, your opponent will relax for a brief moment. While he is relaxed, attack him with full force.

- **Intensity of feints**

  Execute a number of attacks rather weakly and half-heartedly thus tricking the opponent into expecting that nothing will come from you. Then start a strong attack, which will become a rather unpleasant surprise for the opponent.

  This category also includes cases where you don't fully complete some techniques. You pretend that you cannot reach your opponent from a certain distance. If you then use the full amplitude of the technique, the opponent will be hit and he won't know why.

  The same basic pattern is also valid for slow and fast attacks. Several relatively slow attacks cause the opponent to assess your speed incorrectly. If you then attack normally, you will surprise him.

- **Spatial feints**

  Here we mention only a few options to illustrate the principle:
  - High-low and vice versa.
  - Right-left and vice versa.
  - Inside-outside and vice versa.

2.2.6.2 Mae-geri

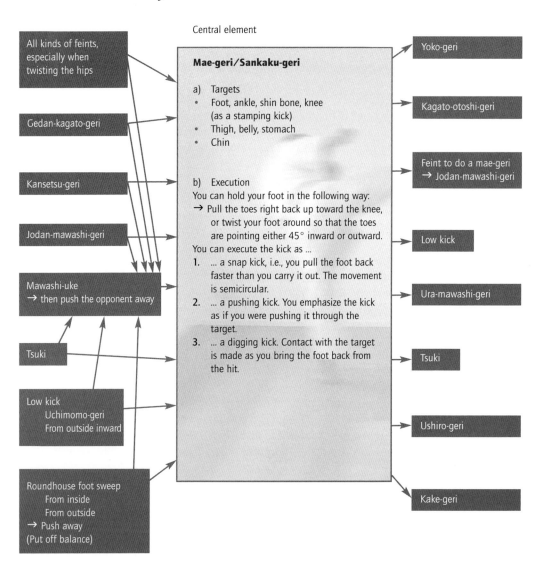

Central element

All kinds of feints, especially when twisting the hips

Gedan-kagato-geri

Kansetsu-geri

Jodan-mawashi-geri

Mawashi-uke
→ then push the opponent away

Tsuki

Low kick
   Uchimomo-geri
   From outside inward

Roundhouse foot sweep
   From inside
   From outside
→ Push away
(Put off balance)

Mae-geri/Sankaku-geri

a) Targets
- Foot, ankle, shin bone, knee
  (as a stamping kick)
- Thigh, belly, stomach
- Chin

b) Execution
You can hold your foot in the following way:
→ Pull the toes right back up toward the knee, or twist your foot around so that the toes are pointing either 45° inward or outward.
You can execute the kick as ...
1. ... a snap kick, i.e., you pull the foot back faster than you carry it out. The movement is semicircular.
2. ... a pushing kick. You emphasize the kick as if you were pushing it through the target.
3. ... a digging kick. Contact with the target is made as you bring the foot back from the hit.

Yoko-geri

Kagato-otoshi-geri

Feint to do a mae-geri
→ Jodan-mawashi-geri

Low kick

Ura-mawashi-geri

Tsuki

Ushiro-geri

Kake-geri

Using a mae-geri, you create a relatively large distance to your opponent. Therefore, we recommend that you use the mae-geri as the last technique in a combination or series. The same is valid for the yoko-geri.

Diagram 23

Mae-geri at the opponent's pelvis optimally at right angles.

The mae-geri doesn't connect.

When you cannot strike at right angles, your mae-geri slips easily away from the partner's body. If the partner knows this, he turns sideways to avoid your mae-geri.

In a fight or sparring, the fighters are almost never aligned in a parallel stance. Therefore, even your best-executed mae-geri will almost never be optimal. You must therefore take up a position that allows you to deliver a mae-geri at the proper angle. A second option: Modify the mae-geri into a sankaku-geri. (The sankaku-geri is a mixture of mae-geri and mawashi-geri. It is executed at a 45° angle from the outside.)

Mae-geri is not delivered correctly.

Alternative: Sankaku-geri.

Target areas:

Mae-geri is turned into an uchi-geri (kicked from the inside to the outside in order to hit the target optimally).

Uchi-geri at the head

Short distance

Mae-geri done at short distance. Keep the hips to the rear and kick under the cover.

A shoving kick. You create distance for the next technique. Important: Kick diagonally (right foot aims at the opponent's right hand side).

Specifically in self-defense, you should use the following kick:

Turn your foot outward and kick with the sole or the inside edge of the foot. Caution: Turn the foot of the supporting leg inward also so you remain stable.
Also for self-defense: The so-called "digging" kick. The special feature of this kick only works when you draw your leg backwards.

Kick well behind the target.   Pull the leg back and up from behind.

The next version shows the mae-geri with the fighter performing a punch as he places his foot down:

When shortening the time, the punch occurs during the withdrawal phase of the kicking foot. This opposing movement causes a strengthening of the punch (see the "Principle of countermovement – biomechanics"). The person attacked cannot cope with the speed of the successive move.

Further chains of action:

Feint using faked technique

Disturb the balance by sweeping with the outside of the ankle or the outside edge of the foot (rather unusual version)

The same leg delivers a mae-geri

And finally:

2.2.6.3   Hiza-geri

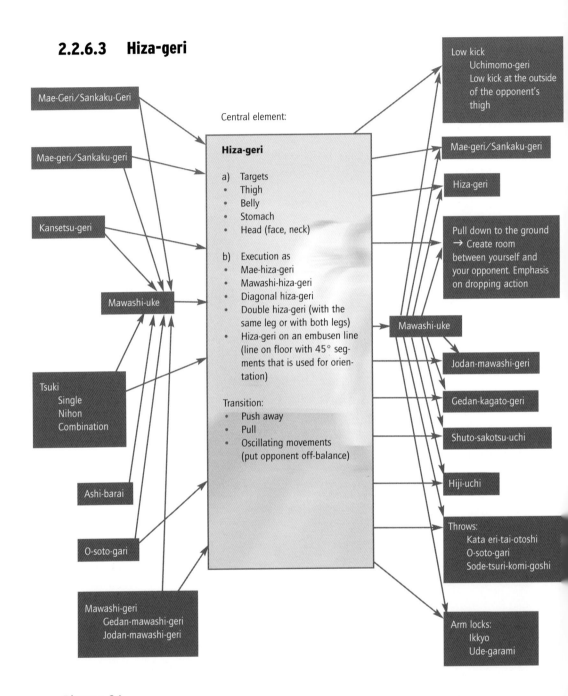

Mae-Geri/Sankaku-Geri

Mae-geri/Sankaku-geri

Kansetsu-geri

Mawashi-uke

Tsuki
Single
Nihon
Combination

Ashi-barai

O-soto-gari

Mawashi-geri
Gedan-mawashi-geri
Jodan-mawashi-geri

Central element:

Hiza-geri

a)   Targets
• Thigh
• Belly
• Stomach
• Head (face, neck)

b)   Execution as
• Mae-hiza-geri
• Mawashi-hiza-geri
• Diagonal hiza-geri
• Double hiza-geri (with the same leg or with both legs)
• Hiza-geri on an embusen line (line on floor with 45° segments that is used for orientation)

Transition:
• Push away
• Pull
• Oscillating movements (put opponent off-balance)

Low kick
Uchimomo-geri
Low kick at the outside of the opponent's thigh

Mae-geri/Sankaku-geri

Hiza-geri

Pull down to the ground
→ Create room between yourself and your opponent. Emphasis on dropping action

Mawashi-uke

Jodan-mawashi-geri

Gedan-kagato-geri

Shuto-sakotsu-uchi

Hiji-uchi

Throws:
Kata eri-tai-otoshi
O-soto-gari
Sode-tsuri-komi-goshi

Arm locks:
Ikkyo
Ude-garami

Diagram 24

Hiza-geri is one of the key close combat techniques. So that the fighter can efficiently deliver the technique, he must:

- Be in the right position

- Be at the right distance

- Correctly use the body mechanics, i.e., push of the hips, direction of force with the knee kick, possibly pulling the opponent into the technique to reinforce it

- Be able to deliver a powerful knee kick at all angles, starting straight from their own body position

Starting from a controlling grip ...

... the fighter can deliver the hiza-geri at all target levels.

By holding the opponent's kicking leg, the "target area" remains open.

Various ways of executing:

Done in a straight line with the arms counterbalancing

Done as a mawashi-hiza-geri

This version comes from Muay Thai. From a clinch situation, the fighter pulls his knee high up to one side and strikes with the inside of his knee at the short ribs of his opponent using a sharp inward rotation of the hips.

At the beginning of this chapter, we wrote that the fighter should be able to deliver a powerful hiza-geri in all directions from his body position. We now present the form of exercise he can use to train for it.

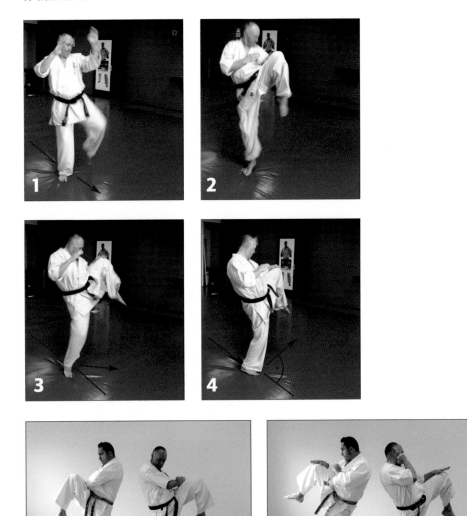

The kick shown once again at a 90° angle. But here the fighter draws the target into the kick.

The hiza-geri after turning round 180°.

Starting the movement for the 180° turn.

Once again, the hiza-geri, done here with a jump

Chains of actions with a hiza-geri:

Change of position

A further one:

Use the opponent's circular movement to execute a knee kick. Continuing the circular motion.

Push the opponent away from you and take up an on-guard position.

And yet another alternative:

After deflecting the mae-geri, take hold of the opponent's shoulder with your right hand.

Because you are attacking a training partner as he falls, we recommend that for safety reasons (namely your partner's), you place your foot where his head comes down. (If you incorrectly assess the rate of fall, you can hurt your partner badly.)

The next move:

Follow-up strikes

Hand changes. Standard rule: One hand controls, the other strikes.

In other words: One hand is always holding the opponent.

By moving your weight over suddenly and with a simultaneous sharp tug of the hands diagonally down to the ground, you will pull the opponent down to the ground.

2.2.6.4 Low Kick

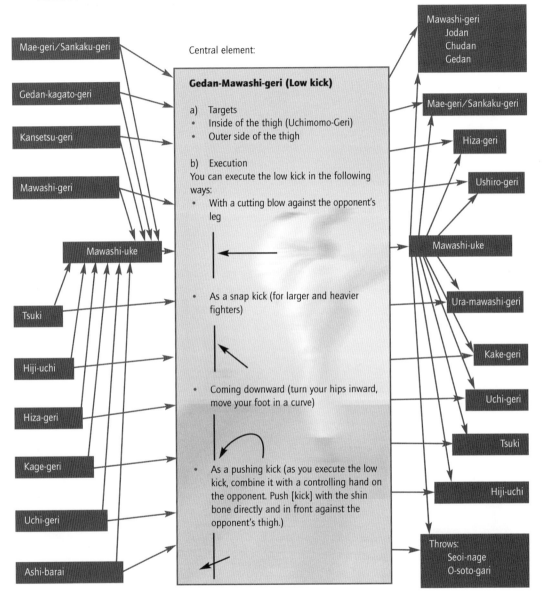

Mae-geri/Sankaku-geri

Gedan-kagato-geri

Kansetsu-geri

Mawashi-geri

Mawashi-uke

Tsuki

Hiji-uchi

Hiza-geri

Kage-geri

Uchi-geri

Ashi-barai

Central element:

Gedan-Mawashi-geri (Low kick)

a)   Targets
   • Inside of the thigh (Uchimomo-Geri)
   • Outer side of the thigh

b)   Execution
You can execute the low kick in the following ways:
   • With a cutting blow against the opponent's leg

   • As a snap kick (for larger and heavier fighters)

   • Coming downward (turn your hips inward, move your foot in a curve)

   • As a pushing kick (as you execute the low kick, combine it with a controlling hand on the opponent. Push [kick] with the shin bone directly and in front against the opponent's thigh.)

Mawashi-geri
Jodan
Chudan
Gedan

Mae-geri/Sankaku-geri

Hiza-geri

Ushiro-geri

Mawashi-uke

Ura-mawashi-geri

Kake-geri

Uchi-geri

Tsuki

Hiji-uchi

Throws:
Seoi-nage
O-soto-gari

Diagram 25

In the early '60s, Kyokushin Karate was confronted with the Muay Thai style. At that time, the Kyokushin Karatekas had adopted the low kick into their technical repertoire. The low kick, as part of effective combinations, is used to disrupt but may also be a decisive technique. Because of its short trajectory, it is also difficult to block. It can be combined with all techniques and is one of the most versatile techniques in Full Contact Karate.

Using a short uchimomo-geri, you lift the opponent's leg outward.

Controlling grip

Low kick

Uchimomo-geri from a different perspective

Hook-kick with the heel. "Hack" your heel with a circular sweep against the outside of the opponent's thigh (also known as a "Charley horse")

You can attack both legs with a low kick

Using a low kick, you can get yourself and your partner into an excellent position to deliver a hook to the liver.

Using a diagonal step forward, you leave the direct combat line ...

... and applying a sharp twist of the hips, you attack your opponent with a sweeping kick/low kick at his calves.

Starting position for ...

... a pushing low kick.

Push kick version

In the next version, twisting your hips well in, you strike against the opponent's thigh using your shin bone moving down from top to bottom. Because of the angle of impact, the muscles on the outside of the thigh are lengthened abruptly. This leads to a protective reflex by the muscles. This causes the opponent to bend sharply back.

In conclusion, here is a form for the low kick:

> Take on and absorb the energy from the low kick. This means you hold the shin bone elastically so that the energy from the opponent's kick partly evaporates.

Direct the counterattack with a low kick using the other leg

Place the blocking leg down, take a short step to change over (kosa-ho) and deliver a low kick with the same leg.

2.2.6.5 Mawashi-geri

The mawashi-geri came into existence out of the need to get around the opponent's cover. It is a versatile technique because you can start from different approaches and from various angles of attack. The technique gets its penetrating power from the fact that as you execute it, you twist your hips well in and fix the position of the standing leg precisely on the ground.

A demonstration of the gedan-mawashi-geri can be found in Chapter 2.2.6.4 "Low kick." For a description of the units of action for the mawashi-geri, we refer you likewise to those for the low kicks.

Middle kicking height: Chudan-mawashi-geri.
We show the following three different ways of leading up to the kick.

The initial movement in the mawashi-geri is identical with that of the mae-geri. This keeps the opponent uncertain about the exact trajectory of the kick until the last moment.

By twisting the standing leg and pushing the hips forward ...

... the mawashi-geri kick lands at the right angle.

The advantages of the following classic lead-up movements are that you work on the mobility of your hips, you develop great penetrating power by virtue of the long trajectory and you can develop an awareness of your specific body mechanics for this kick. In our opinion, the disadvantages largely outweigh the benefits. As you can see in the first two pictures, you open your abdominal area for a long period of time to the opponent's attacks. Since the mawashi-geri has a curved path of movement, a straight-line attack at the opponent, carried out resolutely, is always quicker to hit the target than a mawashi-geri.

Lift your leg up high sideways, twist the standing leg and hips around inward with one large movement. The kick is almost parallel to the ground.

In the third version, you hold a position for the real kick in the direction that you chose later. This initial motion can deceive the enemy since he does not expect a mawashi-geri.

An example of the mawashi-geri from the outside line. Kick under the attacking arm.

In the following series, both fighters start in a close combat situation.

Freeing and pushing using shotei

Kick

How do you defend against a jodan-mawashi-geri?

The option shown here consists of catching the mawashi-geri with a double-block and sweeping the attacking leg down to the ground with the hand.

Dry run

In the next sequence, the fighter executes a double-kick without placing his foot down in-between.

Further examples:

2.2.6.6 Ushiro-geri

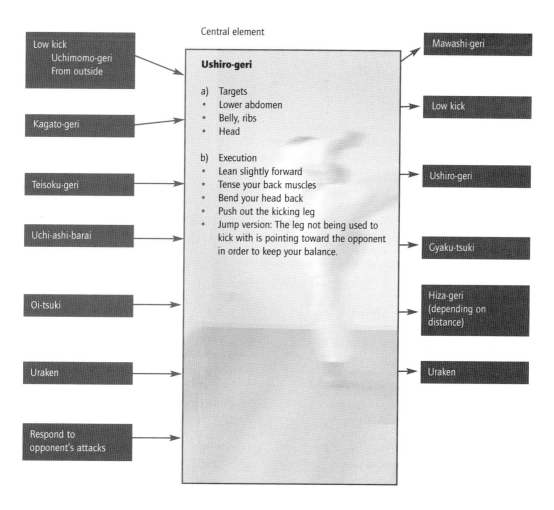

Central element

Low kick
  Uchimomo-geri
  From outside

Kagato-geri

Teisoku-geri

Uchi-ashi-barai

Oi-tsuki

Uraken

Respond to
opponent's attacks

Ushiro-geri

a) Targets
  • Lower abdomen
  • Belly, ribs
  • Head

b) Execution
  • Lean slightly forward
  • Tense your back muscles
  • Bend your head back
  • Push out the kicking leg
  • Jump version: The leg not being used to
    kick with is pointing toward the opponent
    in order to keep your balance.

Mawashi-geri

Low kick

Ushiro-geri

Gyaku-tsuki

Hiza-geri
(depending on
distance)

Uraken

Diagram 26

The traditional version of the ushiro-geri requires that the knee is brought first up to the chest and then kicked to the rear. The advantage of a longer path of movement (more force development) is, however, dissipated by the fact that the movement forward and upward is stopped and then has to be transferred into a counter-movement. This can lead to an abrupt hyperextension of the lumbar spine, which we believe is not very safe. Therefore, we recommend the following modified version.

By lifting up the heel, the thigh is tensed and this tension is transferred into the stretched kicking leg.

Hit by an ushiro-geri

Doing the ushiro-geri from a short distance. Note: Keep your center of balance low.

Jump version:

Another use:

Above: After executing a gyaku-tsuki, place your weight over the rear right leg and combine this move with a sweeping kick with the inside of the foot.

Left: Twist around the axis of your body and execute an ushiro-geri.

Ushiro-geri executed as a counterattack, simultaneously from a turn.

Here, we show two examples of follow-up actions for the ushiro-geri.

Above: The fighter feints an ushiro-geri and at the same time anticipates the opponent's evading movement. He breaks off from the movement of the ushiro-geri ...

Left: ... and ends the action with a form of yoko-geri/ushiro-geri in the direction of his opponent.

A similar version:

The opponent lengthens the distance and the fighter prepares for a counterattack.

Anticipation of the counterattack and counter using uraken.

Close-up view

A close-combat version seldom used:

2.2.6.7   Tsuki

First, a demonstration of an oi-tsuki/kizami-tsuki (jab):

The punch is accompanied with an adjusting step forward so that the body weight increases the punch.

General rule: Each fist technique is combined with a shift of your weight (translation and/or rotation).

In Full Contact Karate without hand protectors, it is extremely important that you choose the right technique in relation to the position of the fist. Fists are extremely vulnerable (in contrast to popular opinion) by virtue of the "soft" hand bones. This is also true even for "tough guys." While a boxer can afford to hit from almost any angle without injury because of his protection by bandages and padded boxing gloves, this is not possible in Full Contact Karate. Because of the lack of hand protection, it follows logically that the repertoire for punching techniques is limited. Here, we show some of the fist positions and explain their form of usage.

The almost classic form
Pro: The twist of the fist is transferred onto the target according to the traditional theory. **Con:** Danger of snapping the wrist back if not delivered with a right-angled impact.

Fist turned 45°. A frequently used form in the Okinawa styles. **Advantage:** Great stability in the wrist, because the radius and ulna in the forearm are aligned almost parallel above each other.

Fist vertical. Used for close distances. **Advantage:** The fist is turned 45°.

Fist position for hooks to the liver or side of the body

Fist position for punching over the cover (overhook)

Examples of usage:
In a close combat situation using various forms of hooks

Example with a gyaku-tsuki

Example of a vertically held fist punching through cover

A further hook

Usage as a hook to the liver after a defensive double sweeping action

Diverting the gyaku-tsuki attack

Guarding with the right hand

The sweeping action to the left moves fluently into a hook to the liver

2.2.6.8 Other Techniques

In this chapter, we show techniques that are only of secondary importance for the full contact competition. For completeness, we would not wish to leave them out. We will, however, only give a brief overview of them.

Kake-geri:
A nice technique but not without danger to yourself!

Ura-mawashi-geri:

Much penetrating power (when and if it hits the target), but a long distance, loss of eye contact with the opponent and possible danger to yourself!

Kansetsu-geri:

For use in self-defense. Please never use in regular training!

Hiji-uchi:

Elbow techniques, in addition to knee kicks, are the most effective close combat weapons. The structure of the movements involved is almost identical to that of the hook. It is crucial to their effectiveness that you deliver elbow strikes as you do a hook punch, namely with *whole body movements*. For example, do this without the rotation of the body as these techniques do not develop any penetrating power. A helpful visualization: Imagine the rotating movement done when someone stubs out a cigarette by squashing it down under the forefoot with a twist of the hips.

Form of exercise to practice the rotation of the hips for the hiji-uchi:

A sequence to demonstrate the various angles of attack in the hiji-uchi:

Kagato-otoshi-geri:

Andy Hug introduced the axe kick into the full contact scene. Originally coming from Taekwondo, it is a technique that, for the opponent, comes in from an unexpected angle. Prerequisites for its successful use, however, are above-average agility and great speed.

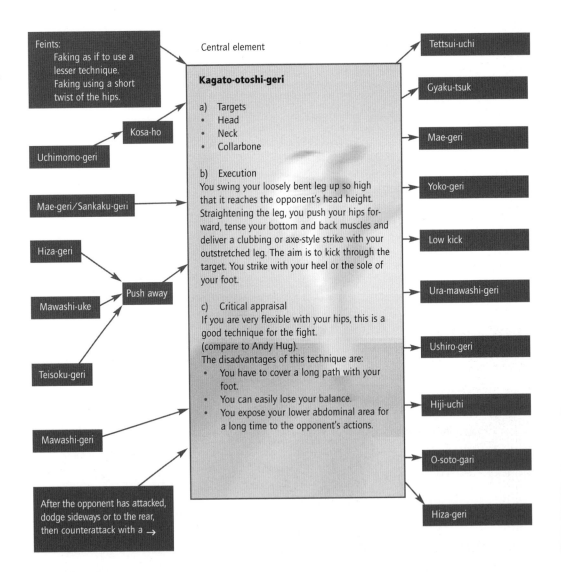

Feints:
Faking as if to use a lesser technique.
Faking using a short twist of the hips.

Kosa-ho

Uchimomo-geri

Mae-geri/Sankaku-geri

Hiza-geri

Push away

Mawashi-uke

Teisoku-geri

Mawashi-geri

After the opponent has attacked, dodge sideways or to the rear, then counterattack with a →

Central element

Kagato-otoshi-geri

a) Targets
• Head
• Neck
• Collarbone

b) Execution
You swing your loosely bent leg up so high that it reaches the opponent's head height. Straightening the leg, you push your hips forward, tense your bottom and back muscles and deliver a clubbing or axe-style strike with your outstretched leg. The aim is to kick through the target. You strike with your heel or the sole of your foot.

c) Critical appraisal
If you are very flexible with your hips, this is a good technique for the fight.
(compare to Andy Hug).
The disadvantages of this technique are:
• You have to cover a long path with your foot.
• You can easily lose your balance.
• You expose your lower abdominal area for a long time to the opponent's actions.

Tettsui-uchi

Gyaku-tsuk

Mae-geri

Yoko-geri

Low kick

Ura-mawashi-geri

Ushiro-geri

Hiji-uchi

O-soto-gari

Hiza-geri

Diagram 27

As the kick in the full contact mode can only be executed properly by exceptionally talented persons, we have not provided a detailed illustration.

An example:

2.2.6.9   Transitional Techniques

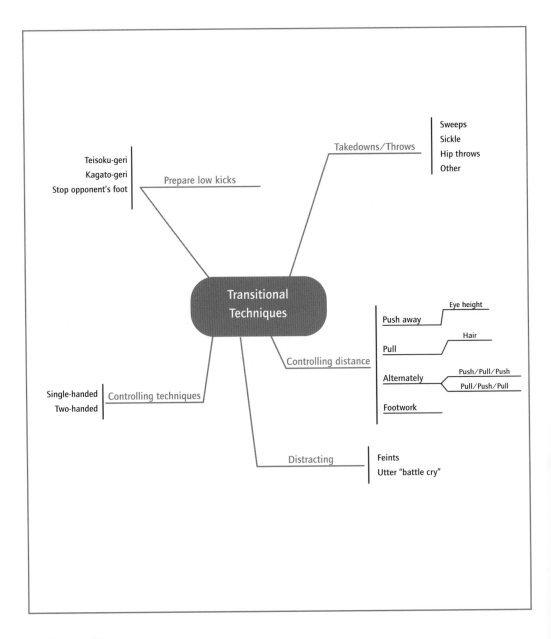

Diagram 28

Transitional techniques have the following functions:

- Preparing for crucial fighting techniques
- Providing for tactical moments within combinations and series
- Controlling the opponent

Examples of use:

An example using the sweeping motion:

There are two opportunities when a sweeping motion can be successfully applied:

- The leg you want to sweep moves forward. This means that the opponent's weight has moved forward. Just before the moving leg touches down, you cause the opponent to take a longer step.

Idea: He's slipped on a banana skin.

- The enemy shifts his weight back. Thus, he has taken the weight off his front leg, which you then sweep away.

Here is a little exercise for this:

At the beginning, discuss who plays which role – one does the sweep, the other lets it happen. Both training partners grab each other (by the arm, lapel, etc.). They both begin to move forward and backwards and eventually find a common rhythm. The goal of the students is to find the exact right time when the opponent has lengthened his step so that the other can do the sweep.

In the last sequence of this section of the chapter, we will show you how to get behind the opponent and throw him.

Sweeping the front leg   The fighter gets behind the opponent

Abrupt lowering of the center of balance while blocking the rear leg

Throw

2.2.6.10 Mawashi-uke

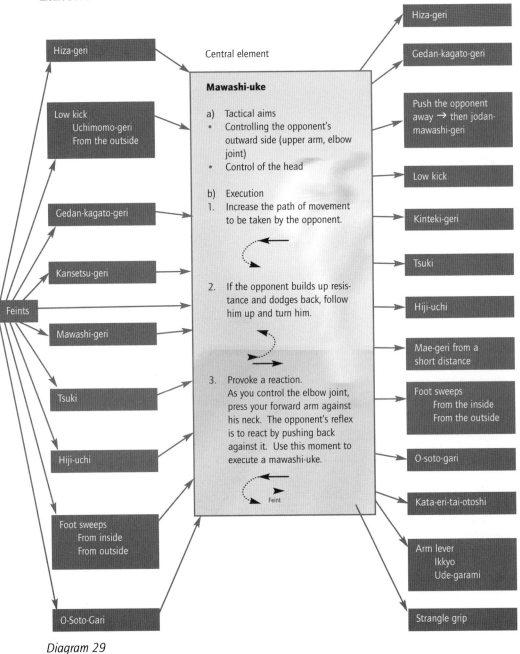

Diagram 29

Mawashi-uke is a controlling grip in which you control the opponent's neck and elbows. This grip allows you to pull the opponent around in a circular motion. This renders him helpless so that you can use a crucial technique.

The basic position

One use of the mawashi-uke

Moving into the two-step turn

The grip position from another perspective

The two-step turn is completed.
The opponent is off-balance.

Get the right distance

"Over and out"

A further usage

The controlling hand circles around the opponent's neck ...

... and presses the head to one side.
Attention: You must keep contact, otherwise you will lose control of the head.

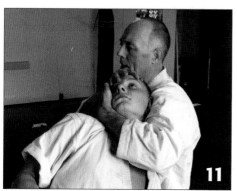

Your right hand takes control of the head. The closeness of the left side of your body to the opponent controls the close contact with him pinning his now-free left arm.

You turn the opponent around and pull him into the following knee technique.

In the following sequence, we show you a turning throw (makikomi-nage) following a mawashi-uke.

Another way of gripping for the mawashi-uke

Another sequence:

Another way of using a transitional technique from a mawashi-uke

2.2.7   Training Plans –
Build-up for the Long-term Fighter

The training plan is a science in itself. The fact is that no one can remain permanently in top form for a long time. When a fighter is preparing for a tournament, his training plan must be built up so that the he reaches the top of his performance at the exact moment he needs – and it is possible to keep this peak for a short time.

The instructor and the student need to analyze together which components of training must be emphasized individually and how they can be integrated in a logical, physiologically appropriate training system. In the long-term planning, the instructor should divide the time before the competition into two or three preparatory periods.

In the first preparatory period (PP1), the focus is on the general principles of training, such as endurance, strength, coordinative skills and learning new techniques and combinations/series (nearing the "complete" fighter). Sparring exercises are not very important in PP1. In the second and third preparatory periods, sparring exercises with specific tasks take up much of the time, without neglecting the fitness and technical basic elements. The closer to the date of the tournament one gets, the greater is the proportion of combat exercises (with specific tasks) and free sparring.

The tactical tasks for the combat training are based on the student's weaknesses and strengths, as well as looking at the fighting style of potential opponents (as much as they are known). If video recordings of previous fights are available, the student should try to develop strategies for a possible fight based on this material. Mental training by the student looking at himself and the potential opponent in the fight, as well as imagining himself as victorious is also a valuable tool. If the feeling arises in the student that he has done everything to prepare for the tournament, then he will enter the fight with confidence.

An important note: It is not a question of training as much possible but training intelligently!

The rest periods are the hours or days after training, in which the training input is digested and converted into growth and improvement. Training for performance power needs to be planned wisely (especially the rest periods). Otherwise, it happens very quickly that the student may slip into a state of over-training. This thwarts all previous efforts.

After the tournament, a recuperation period of 2-3 weeks should be planned in which the fighter trains lightly and recovers. At the end of this period, the cycle begins again at a high level.

The split of these periods is dependent upon a specific structure based on long-term training. For this, we turn to the content of the individual training.

The following list is not exhaustive; it merely gives an overview of what training can be arranged.

Table 2: Split of the training period

Period →		Examples/Description	PP I	PP II	PP III	Competition	Recuperation	PP I	...
Fitness	Warm-up								
	Stamina								
	Power training								
	Flexibility								
	Speed								
	Coordination ability								
	Cool down								
	Cross training	Badminton, running, swimming							
	Recuperation	Sleep, sauna, massage, etc.							
Technical	Shadow/Kick boxing								
	Basic training without partner	Learning new techniques							
	Basic training with partner								
	Standard situations with partner	Recurring situations							
	Partner training – specific tasks								
	Sparring with specific tasks								
	Free sparring								
	Kata training with partner								
	Self-defense training								
Mental	Observation training	When injured, under supervision							
	Visualization training	I go through techniques and combinations in my head and aim at a training effect							
	Psychological training	I learn how to put the instructor's words into practice and make up key words/phrases that I must react to							

2.2.7.1 Fitness Elements of Training

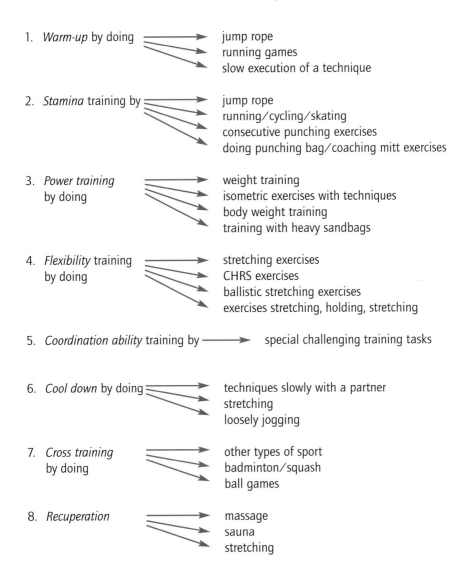

1. *Warm-up* by doing → jump rope
   running games
   slow execution of a technique

2. *Stamina* training by → jump rope
   running/cycling/skating
   consecutive punching exercises
   doing punching bag/coaching mitt exercises

3. *Power training* by doing → weight training
   isometric exercises with techniques
   body weight training
   training with heavy sandbags

4. *Flexibility* training by doing → stretching exercises
   CHRS exercises
   ballistic stretching exercises
   exercises stretching, holding, stretching

5. *Coordination ability* training by → special challenging training tasks

6. *Cool down* by doing → techniques slowly with a partner
   stretching
   loosely jogging

7. *Cross training* by doing → other types of sport
   badminton/squash
   ball games

8. *Recuperation* → massage
   sauna
   stretching

2.2.7.2   Technical Elements of Training

1. Shadow boxing
2. Kihon *without* a partner (emphasis is on the *correct body mechanics and precise movement paths*)
3. Kihon with partner (partner is cooperative, focus is on the *correct distance, impact angle, footwork, target precision*)
4. Kihon *with* partner (partner has an *active role* defined by the instructor)
5. Sparring with tactical tasks
6. Free sparring
7. Kata training (focus more on the *technical* or the *fitness* element)
8. Self-defense training

2.2.7.3   Mental Training

1. Observation training (watching, visiting other schools and dojos)
2. Visualization (I imagine how I would execute techniques and combinations and aim at a training effect)
3. Psychological training (putting the instructor's tips into practice, using key words or phrases)

The improvement of fighting ability is the supreme goal of all these training measures. About 85-95% of the sparring exercises should include tactical tasks. Using this format allows the student to learn better. He develops more effective behavioral patterns and improves his technical/tactical ability. The fact that the instructor sets practical tasks, means he can tailor the training program to fit the student. He can then make progress according to his personal abilities.

As the competition approaches, the more free sparring training the fighter should complete. His training partner has to try to imitate the fighting style of potential opponents. For the serious fighter, it is important to plan the training periods. We strongly recommend that as a competitor, you keep a training diary. If you write down your training content, you can understand the reasons why you had successes or failures. At the same time, writing down your content, your body's reactions and emotions, it serves as a little education exercise for the disciplined pursuit of your training goals!

An example of how such a training diary may look as a weekly plan is on the next page. It is very similar to the format shown above. Our example is only a suggestion. You are welcome to develop your own format to suit your personal needs! Have fun and write often!

Table 3: The weekly training plan

		Mon	Tues	Wed	Thurs	Fri	Sat	Sun
	Time							
	Content							
Fitness	Warm-up							
	Stamina							
	Power training							
	Flexibility							
	Speed							
	Coordination ability							
	Cool down							
	Cross training							
	Recuperation							
	Other							
Technical	Shadow/Kick boxing							
	Basic training without partner							
	Basic training with partner							
	Standard situations with partner							
	Partner training – specific tasks							
	Sparring with specific tasks							
	Free sparring							
	Kata training with partner							
	Self-defense training							
	Other							
Mental	Observation training							
	Visualization training							
	Psychological training							
	Other							

The training diary can be derived from these categories in the weekly planning. It can also contain information on body weight, diet, sleep, and one's feelings, both during and after training. If the athlete is forced to keep a written record seriously, he can detect errors and prevent them from occurring in his training.

We also recommend that you maintain a diary about your diet. In addition to the quantities of fluid and food intake, you should answer and record the following questions:

* *What time* do you eat or drink?
* *What* do you eat and drink?
* *How much?*
* *Why?*
* Possible reasons: The food was readily available (cookie jar on the table, fast-food restaurant on the way home, etc.), was hungry, etc.
* *How?*
  It makes no difference if I eat standing up or sit down to a well-decorated table with a sumptuous meal.

A diary kept like this will allow the instructor and the fighter to uncover weaknesses and areas for improvement. Whenever the fighter looks in his diary, it will usually have an eye-opening effect in stark black and white. Often, the fighter knows enough about nutrition.

Together, instructors and students set goals that need to be adjusted again after time. By using the training target definitions, training progress can be measured. It is like chess: Here again, the tool is not only the body, but the brain also!

Again:
The winner is not the fighter who trains the most.
The winner is the one who trains intelligently!

Literature

In the selection of literature that follows, we have taken quite a subjective point of view. If any avid reader feels we have missed any major titles, then we would be very grateful to know about it. The books listed go deeper into aspects that we may have only touched on in this work. Again, as in other areas of life, expanding your horizons through reading never hurts. Have fun browsing!

Anderson, D. (1980). *American Freestyle Karate:* A Guide to Sparring. Hollywood, CA: Unique Publications.

Ashihara, H. (1991). *Fighting Karate* (5th Edition). Tokyo: Kodansha America, Inc.

Ashihara, H. (1989). *More Fighting Karate.* Tokyo: Kodansha America, Inc.

Hassell, R. G. (1985). "On the Hard Way." *Black Belt: The World's Leading Magazine of Martial Arts.* March 1985, pp. 96-112.

Kent, C. & Tackett T. (1988). *Jeet Kune Do Kickboxing.* Los Angeles, CA: Beckett Publications.

Kuk, H. C., Sang, H. K. & Kyung, M. L. (1994). *Taekwondo Kyorugi: Olympic Style Sparring.* Wethersfield, CT: Turtle Press.

Lovret, F. J. (1987). *The Way and the Power: Secrets of Japanese Strategy.* Boulder, CO: Paladin Press.

Ninomiya, J. (1998). *Sabaki Method: Karate in the Inner Circle.* Berkeley, CA: Frog Books.

O'Keeffe, P. (1999). *Kickboxing: A Framework for Success.* Chichester: Summersdale.

O'Keeffe, Pat (2002). *Advanced Kickboxing.* Chichester: Summersdale Publisher.

Rabesa, A. (1986). *Kumite: The Complete Fighting Text.* Brockton, MA: Peabody Publishing.

Photo & Illustration Credits:

Cover photos: Axel Maluschka, © fotolia/MAXFX, © fotolia/Eduard
Cover design: Sabine Groten
Internal photos: Axel Maluschka

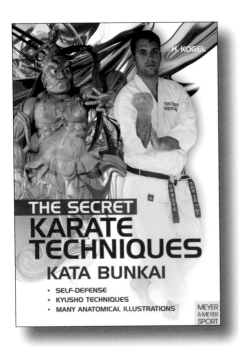

Helmut Kogel
The Secret Karate Techniques
Kata Bunkai

The varied facets of Karate first become obvious to the Karate student after many years of intensive training and study of the roots of Okinawa's Martial Arts. This book guides you through the theoretical and historical background and the practice of the so-called secret techniques.

248 p., full-color print, 486 photos, 3 illus.
Paperback, 6 1/2" x 9 1/4"
ISBN: 9781841262895
$ 19.95 US/$ 32.95 AUS/£ 14.95 UK/€ 19.95

Joachim Grupp
Shotokan Karate – Kihon, Kumite, Kata

This manual offers assistance to all Shotokan Karateka to use when training or intensively preparing skills. Kihon techniques, Kumite forms as well as free-fighting and basic Katas are described in detail. This is a complete package for those wishing to improve themselves.

2nd, revised edition
160 p., full-color, more than 400 photos
Paperback, 6 1/2" x 9 1/4"
ISBN: 9781841262819
$ 17.95 US/$ 29.95 AUS/£ 12.95 UK/€ 16.95

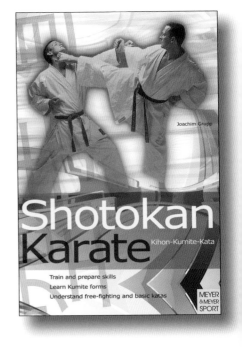

All books available as E-books.

- secure & user-friendly

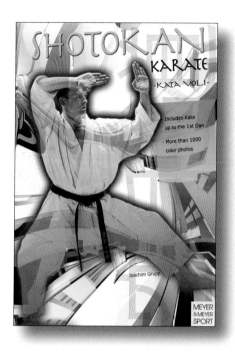

Joachim Grupp
Shotokan Karate Kata Vol. 1

The Kata are the backbone of Karate. Continually practicing them allows the whole spectrum of possibilities contained in Karate to be revealed. They consist of a multitude of techniques, which permit defense in close contact as well as at medium and long distance.

2nd, revised edition
216 pages, full-color print
965 photos, 13 illus., Paperback, 6 1/2" x 9 1/4"
ISBN: 9781841262826
$ 19.95 US/$ 32.95 AUS/£ 14.95 UK/€ 18.95

Joachim Grupp
Shotokan Karate Kata Vol. 2

The master Kata described in this book belong to the advanced repertoire and carry on from the Kata introduced in Volume 1. There are 9 Shotokan Kata with Bunkai in this book, completing the list: Sochin, Meikyo, Chinte, Kanku-Sho, Wankan, Ji'in, Jitte, Gankaku, and Unsu.

2nd edition

152 pages, two-color print, 682 photos
Paperback, 6 1/2" x 9 1/4"
ISBN: 9781841260914
$ 17.95 US/$ 29.95 AUS/£ 12.95 UK/€ 16.90

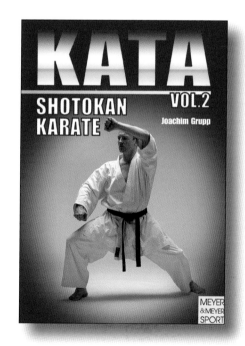

■ online
www.m-m-sports.com

■ E-Mail
sales@m-m-sports.com

MEYER
& MEYER
SPORT